SHADOW BR

GEORGE SWEET

www.dizzyemupublishing.com

DIZZY EMU PUBLISHING

1714 N McCadden Place, Hollywood, Los Angeles 90028

www.dizzyemupublishing.com

Shadow Brother

George Sweet

ISBN: 9781549971099

First published in the United States

in 2017 by Dizzy Emu Publishing

www.dizzyemupublishing.com

Shadow Brother

by

George Sweet

FADE IN:

EXT. MOIR WOODS, SAN FRANCISCO AREA (NIGHT) - OUTLINE OF GRAND HOUSE ON SKYLINE - SHOWING OBLONG OF SINGLE YELLOW LIGHTED WINDOW

PANTING BREATHING of WATCHER, the House as viewed eighty to hundred yards from his hidden position in doorway of PAVILION, not seen at this point.

An arc of sulphurous lamplight spreads some fifteen feet from the Pavilion. Silhouettes of tall trees are evident in the surround and stars and a gibbous moon can be seen above the House.

A slant of yellow light cuts from the house, and a moment later a SHADOW FIGURE rises and elongates as in a Disney cartoon as Figure walks toward Watcher, who snickers and then reaches for the hand-axe propped to his naked leg.

At back of him a record bursts into the night:

This from an old scratchy 78 - JOHNNY RAY and TALK TO HER MISTER SUN:

> - - *"Talk to her ple-ease,*
> *Mi-ster Su-un - - Speak to*
> *her, Mister Rainbow - - "*

Johnny's moping voice continues to throb as Shadow Figure nears.

> *"- - And take her under your*
> *branches, Mi-is-ter Tree-ees - -"*

Watcher's panting breath has becomes heavier, as if in fear, as the approaching Figure then becomes whole and a MAN walks casually into the arc of the lamplight.

This is CREIGHTON DOW. He is slim, about forty, and he is wearing a tuxedo. He comes to a halt and glances around in a smug, bored kind of way.

> *" - Whisper to he-er, Mister Wind.*
> *Sing to her, Mister Robin - - "*

>   WATCHER (O.S.)
>   (calling lowly)
> Oh, Brother - - Over here - -

Creighton turns toward Watcher's voice, his gaze moving over the figure he is seeing with contempt.

> *" - - And Miss-as Moonlight, put*
> *in a word fo-or me-ee - - "*

1

                    CREIGHTON
          Am I supposed to make a comparison?
              (frowning)
          What is wrong with you? Why are
          you staring like that? You look
          like a sick toad - - and what's
          this nonsense?

                    WATCHER (O.S.)
          One of the old favourites, remember?

                    CREIGHTON
          Is that what it is?

He begins fixing a cigarette into a long holder.

Watcher's hand tight-grips the axe.

               " - _It shouldn't end-a th-is way - - "

Creighton turns, his face enlarging with shock as hear SWISH OF AXE.

                                        CROSSFADE TO:

SAME - SOME MINUTES LATER

Swirl of trees, stars and moon, Watcher's heavy panting.

               " - - And watch to see they all do - -
               Pe-le-ase Mis-ter Suuun - - "

The creaky ballad reaches its conclusion with high camp relish, the syrupy
boy and girl chorus joining with heartfelt support.

Watcher's breathing slows. Hear the hiss of the needle on the 78 record.
Then see:

PAVILION

This a white marble construct, about twelve feet high, with domed roof and
elaborate minarets adorned on each wing in arabesque style.

Watcher moves toward the open doors and enters.

INT. PAVILION

Close to the door there is an old bell-horn phonograph, the arm of the
needle box swishing back and forth over the 78 record as it grinds down.

Watcher lifts off the needle and from his roving gaze see a swirl of framed
pictures lining the circular wall, a frieze of cherubs rimming the domed
ceiling, a giant-fronded sunflower chandelier.

Watcher's breathing continues to slow as he turns and exits the Pavilion.

EXT. AS BEFORE

In flash see a NAKED BODY, a blurred BATTERED HEAD.

A sob breaks from Watcher. He then bursts out with a triumphant laugh,
which dips becoming a gleeful chuckle.

As quickly the chuckle disappears and from his p.o.v. see:

DARK HOUSE WITH ELEVATED LIGHTED YELLOW WINDOW.

Watcher goes forward, pausing to collect the discarded axe. Moving, he again begins to pant as he blunders toward the House - -

                                                    DISSOLVE TO:

EXT. MURDER SCENE - LATER SAME NIGHT

High-powered spotlights illuminate police and medical personnel as they move around in desultory fashion. A green tent-like apparatus is presumed to cover the corpse. GLEESON, a local detective, 52, heavy-set and silver haired, is engaged in conversation with KLEIN the chief ME, 64, short and bald-headed, somewhat self-important.

                         KLEIN
             - - give you more when I
             get him on the slab.
               (head shaking)
             In all my years - -

He stops as NASH walks up to join them. Nash will be mid- to late-thirties, good-looking with an athlete build and confident manner. Addresses Gleeson:

                         NASH
             Gleeson?
               (flashes his
               ID)

                         GLEESON
             Nash. I've heard of you.

                         NASH
               (to Klein)
             In all your years - - go on,
             Doc, let's have the song and
             dance.

                         KLEIN
             Doctor Klein, if you don't
             mind! And this I assure you
             is no song and dance.
               (frowns questioningly
               at Gleeson)

                         GLEESON
             Inspector Nash is here from the
             City at our request.

                         KLEIN
             Well - - Inspector Nash from the
             City - - for your information
             I was about to say that I have
             never before encountered such
             unbridled fury.

                         NASH
             That so?

                                                         3

                    KLEIN
          That is so. Skull and pretty
          much the whole face bashed in.
          Simply horrendous.

                    NASH
          And it's solid he used an axe?

                    KLEIN
          Heavy instrument, cutting edge,
          what would you say? Started with
          a blow to the side of the head.
          Blade driven hard above the left
          ear. Used it on his genitals, after
          he finished mashing him. Sliced
          the penis as clean as you like
          from the scrotum.

                    NASH
          With an axe?

                    KLEIN
          No, no, that would be quite
          impossible. Something keenly
          sharp, a scalpel more like.
          Took the member with him, a
          trophy maybe. Make of that
          what you will.

Nash walks to the tent and pulls back a flap. Klein follows much agitated,
Gleeson trailing behind.

                    KLEIN
          We haven't finished up yet - -

                    NASH
               (peering in)
          Messy. Can you turn him over?

                    KLEIN
          What is it you want to know?

                    NASH
               (straightening)
          I want to know if he'd lost
          his cherry.

                    GLEESON
          Gay killing, you think? He is,
          or was married, for what it's
          worth.

Nash grunts and gazes out into the blackness seeing flashlights moving.

                    NASH
          What odds come the dawn we're
          set to find a second body out
          in these woods?

Gleeson pulls down his mouth, agreeing.

                    NASH
          A maid's gone missing too,
          that right?

                    GLEESON
               (nods)
          Mexican woman. Their only servant.

                    NASH
          So maybe a full house.

Turns with a mischievous smile as Klein heaves a sigh

                    NASH
          What's-a-matter, Doc? Know what
          they say. Love your work.

                    KLEIN
          Ha!

He hustles away not appreciating the rib. Nash grins and slides out a
spirit flask and takes a belt, switching his gaze to the Pavilion.

                    NASH
          They meet up - - all nice and
          friendly - - reaches for one
          of his fancy custom-made Turkish
          cigarettes - -

                    GLEESON
          What about it being the work of
          a psycho with a grudge?

Nash offers the flask, stowing it away when Gleeson fails to respond.

                    NASH
          The grudge I go along with,
          you have to. But he knew his
          killer. Why else walk all the
          way down here - - midnight - -
          Saturday?
               (nods at the tent)
          What do know about him?

                    GLEESON
          Creighton Dow? I wouldn't know
          if he walked on his toes, if
          that's what you mean. I guess
          you'd call him a playboy. Son
          of old Zachary Dow, if you
          remember him.

                    NASH
          The oil magnate. One hard old
          bastard, judging by the heavyweight
          picture stuck in the house back
          there.
               (beat)
          Isn't there a sister? A kind of
          down-market movie star?

                              GLEESON
                    Veronica Dow, you mean? Yes. Built
                    a name of sorts on the porno horror
                    circuit a while back. She was quite
                    a girl. Ended up marrying some Greek
                    shipping tycoon - -

Nash digests this, reaching again for his flask, as DISSOLVE TO:

RINGING TELEPHONE

INT. HOTEL BEDROOM

VERONICA props up in bed, a phone to her ear. This is Creighton's sister.
She is an attractive woman in her thirties, sinewy with short-cropped dyed
jet-black hair.

We hear VOICE on the line say, "Hello Verro."

                              VERONICA
                    Creighton?

Previously heard effeminate and excited voice of Creighton Dow answers:

                              CREIGHTON (V.O.)
                    I have just pulled off a most
                    amazing feat!
                         (giggling)
                    I have murdered myself.

Veronica flops back on her pillow and closes her eyes.

INT. SHABBY HOTEL ROOM - CONTINUOUS

From Creighton's p.o.v. on his bed see flashing neon light through window.

                              CREIGHTON (V.O.)
                    Did you hear what I said, Verro.
                    I said - -

INT. VERONICA'S BEDROOM

                              VERONICA
                    I heard you! I was dead asleep.
                    How did you know I was here?

INT. CREIGHTON'S BEDROOM - FLASHING WINDOW FROM HIS POV LYING ON THE BED

                              CREIGHTON (V.O.)
                    Just in from gay Paree? Where else
                    would one expect to find my indulgent
                    little sister than the good old Ritz?
                    I'm miffed, all the same. You might
                    have let on you were winging your
                    way homeward.

INT. VERONICA'S BEDROOM

                              VERONICA
                    I - I intended to call - - tomorrow. I'm
                    jet-lagged - - can't keep my eyes open.

                                                                    6

INT. CREIGHTON'S BEDROOM - FLASHING WINDOW

                    CREIGHTON (V.O.)
            You are such a liar, Verro, but I
            forgive you. I also have to admit to
            feeling rather jealous. There you
            are swaddled in silken sheets at the
            Ritz-Carlton while I languish in about
            the crummiest of dumps imaginable.

He gives a tittering laugh, and now glimpse Creighton, his image obscured
in darkness, viewed fleetingly as the neon light winks on and off.

                    CREIGHTON
            Actually I am fibbing. This place
            is marvellous - - a bone-fide
            depression area flop house no
            less. Complete would you believe
            with winking neon sign.

INT. VERONICA'S BEDROOM

                    VERONICA
            I'll call you in the morning.

INT. CREIGHTON'S BEDROOM - FLASHING WINDOW

                    CREIGHTON (V.O.)
            You won't be able to - -
                (tittering)
            - - not unless you can get through
            to the spirit world.

INT. VERONICA'S BEDROM

She closes her eyes and sighs heavily, letting him hear it.

INT. CREIGHTON'S BEDROOM - FLASHING WINDOW

                    CREIGHTON (V.O.)
            Think I'm joshing? Like dear Deborah
            you are in for a big surprise. As
            you might guess, she is off gadding
            on one of her - - what shall we say?
            - - one of her nocturnal sojourns.

INT. VERONICA'S BEDROOM

                    VERONICA
            You married her.

INT. CREIGHTON'S BEDROOM - FLASHING WINDOW

                    CREIGHTON (V.O.)
            How true, and please spare reminding
            me you were right all along - - Oh,
            dear. I hesitate to admit it, but I
            have - - what is that English term?
            - - cocked it up with Chita also.

INT. VERONICA'S BEDROOM

She lies back, eyes closed, enduring his babble.

INT. CREIGHTON'S BEDROOM - FLASHING WINDOW

> CREIGHTON (V.O.)
> The cunning minx second-guessed me
> and made herself heap scarce. Not
> that you can blame her.

INT. VERONICA'S BEDROOM

> VERONICA
> Creighton, I really need to sleep - -

INT. CREIGHTON'S BEDROOM - FLASHING WINDOW

> CREIGHTON (V.O.)
> What? - - yes I suppose you do.

He sighs dramatically, and as before see his obscured flickered image.

> CREIGHTON
> Oh, very well, off you go to
> bye-bye land. I'll be in touch.
> Kiss, kiss, sweet dreams - -

INT. VERONICA'S BEDROOM

She sags exhausted as the call ends. We see her disturbed state, unable to sleep, as DISSOLVE TO:

EXT. SERIES OF MERGING SHOTS - WETTED STREETS - NIGHT

Veronica walking in troubled thought as she passes through a poor area of the city, low-grade buildings and rooming houses in evidence, furry and out of line with reality.

She passes Bay Bridge. Dawn is breaking as she crosses Market Street to the RITZ-CARLTON HOTEL. She climbs steps and goes through into:

LOBBY OF HOTEL

She halts. Two uniform police officers, a male and female, and a plain clothes man stare back at her with the air of those about to impart dreadful news.

> DISSOLVE TO:

INT. MAIN ROOM OF DOW MANSION - GIANT OIL PAINTING OF ZACHARY DOW

The Painting depicts an iron-gray-haired moustachioed man in his middle-ages prime. He is dressed in the manner of an early aviator, jodhpurs, riding boots. One hand is fisted on his hip, elbow outthrust. The other grips a mighty red tome. At back of him idealized white clouds billow over rolling hills, on which are dotted a number of oil derricks.

Nash stares up at the picture. He stands at one far end of a vast high-ceiling open-plan room, this cluttered with art, sculptures, vases, etc.

A wide staircase travels up to the balcony of the first floor. Along from the staircase, a short flight of steps lead up to a wide stage where a baby grand piano with a galaxy of portrait photographs set atop is in evidence. At the back of the stage there is a towering picture window.

Nash walks up onto the stage and crosses to stare out, and from his p.o.v. we see the fading night and distant lights of the City.

After a moment he turns and goes to the baby grand and hits middle C, the note ringing with clarity. He turns to the photographs, moving one to see:

CREIGHTON DOW'S WEDDING PHOTOGRAPH

This is a full works studded tie job. Dow is beanpole thin and shows too many teeth and too little chin. His bride, DEBORAH, is shown to be a beautiful blonde young woman, her stunning good looks emphasized when Nash lifts out and studies her super-large portrait photo.

                    NASH
          Where are you now, beautiful
          Deborah?

He sets the Portrait back and focuses on a second, this of Veronica, who stares back with dramatic intensity.

                    NASH
          I guess you must be Veronica.
          Welcome to the party.

Replacing Veronica's photo, Nash brushes aside a small tarnished silver-framed photo. This has been tucked back from the others as though hidden. He frowns and slides the little picture out to see:

A BLACK-AND-WHITE IMAGE OF TWO FAIR-HAIRED IDENTICAL TWIN BOYS

The boys are about four years old. They are smartly dressed in white sailor suits, their hair parted neatly. They are sharing a ride on a big old-fashioned rocking horse, both boys posing with joyless obedience.

                                        DISSOLVE TO:

INT. PICTURE WINDOW AS BEFORE - EARLY MORNING

Nash stares out drinking coffee as WHITMORE, a young detective, rushes up.

                    WHITMORE
          She's outside!

                    NASH
          What?

                    WHITMORE
          She just drove up. The dead man's
          wife!

                    NASH
          Well get her up here.

                    WHITMORE
          We can't - - the press and TV crews.
          They've gone bats down there.

                              NASH
                          (moving)
                    Shit - -

EXT. GATES FRONTING DOW ESTATE

Nash's car arrives fast at open iron gates, where an oyster-white AMG
Mercedes sportcar (or similar), the black top up, is blocked by a mass of
media people with cameras and mics, shouting - "Mrs Dow - Mrs Dow - "
Behind the wheel, her head tipped forward, eyes downcast, sits Deborah Dow.

Nash battles his way through and raps at the car window, pressing his star
to the glass. After a moment Deborah's head comes around. She has a white
headscarf knotted under her chin. She looks at him, dazed.

Nash mouths at her to open up. She stares bewildered for a moment then nods
and snaps the release button. Nash pushes inside.

                              NASH
                    Move over.

Deborah obeys, squeezing across to the passenger seat. Nash makes a get
back, get-away gesture, and aided by police officers edges the sportcar
through the braying media crowd and drives toward the house.

DRIVE - OUTSIDE DOORS OF HOUSE

The car grinds to a halt.

INTERIOR OF CAR

Nash turns to stare at Deborah, who sits perfectly still, saying after a
beat in an abstracted voice:

                            DEBORAH
                    He is dead - - Creighton.

                              NASH
                    You mean you only just heard?
                    For God's sake, Mrs Dow, your
                    husband's been murdered. There
                    have been calls going out all
                    night trying to trace you.

She makes no response. Nash studies her for a minute then gets out and goes
around to her side of the car, opening the door.

                              NASH
                    Let's get inside.

He helps her out. She staggers against him, and holding her steady he walks
her toward the house.

MAIN LIVING ROOM

Nash guides Deborah to sit at a long kidney-shaped leather couch. He steps
back appraising her. Deborah is deathly pale, staring blankly.

                              NASH
                    Do you want anything? Brandy,
                    some coffee maybe?

Deborah unknots the white headscarf and gives her blonde hair a freeing
shake. Abstracted, not looking at Nash, she says:

                    DEBORAH
          Please tell me what happened.

                    NASH
          Be glad to - - but where have you
          been, Mrs Dow? We were worried
          you had come to harm. Even that
          you had been kidnapped.

                    DEBORAH
          I was out driving.

                    NASH
          Driving, all this time?

                    DEBORAH
          Yes, I sometimes do that - -
          when - when I'm restless.

Nash digests this, warily appraising her.

                    NASH
          That doesn't seem very wise. An
          attractive woman, all alone in
          a high-rated car.

Deborah fishes out a small white hankie to dab at her lips.

                    DEBORAH
          I suppose not.

                    NASH
          Did you have an argument or
          something? - - with your
          husband?

                    DEBORAH
          No, I just knew I wouldn't
          be able to sleep.

                    NASH
          Get wired, I know what you
          mean - - so what time did
          you leave?

                    DEBORAH
          What? Immediately after dinner,
          I think.

                    NASH
          You think?

                    DEBORAH
          Yes, that's right - - around ten
          o'clock. We generally ate late
          Saturday night.

                    NASH
          You were lucky then, Mrs Dow.

                    DEBORAH
          Lucky?

                    NASH
          I would say so. If you hadn't
          left when you did - - well, who
          can say what might have happened.

Deborah turns fixing hard on Nash.

                    DEBORAH
          Please tell me about my husband.

                    NASH
          All right. While you were out cruising,
          some party for reasons so far unknown,
          decided to beat out his brains with
          an axe.

Deborah winces as though she has been struck.

                    DEBORAH
          That is an awful way of telling
          me.

                    NASH
          There is no easy way. And I am
          afraid there is more. The body
          was mutilated - - the private
          parts.

                    DEBORAH
               (sadly shakes
                her head)
          Poor Creighton.

                    NASH
          Yes, I sympathize. Your servant's
          gone missing, too.

                    DEBORAH
          Carmen?

                    NASH
          Is that her name? Yes, she's
          disappeared. I take it she was
          here when you left.

                    DEBORAH
          Why, yes - - what do you suppose - - ?

                    NASH
          Happened to her? We don't know,
          not yet. Could be she witnessed
          the attack and took off. At least
          we hope that's how it turns out.
               (beat)
          Your husband was found out by   (CONT'D)

                                                        12

                         the pavilion - - is that what
                         you call it? Seems he went to
                         meet someone - - Where were you,
                         Mrs Dow?

                                   DEBORAH
                         Like I said - -

                                   NASH
                         Out driving, yes I know. Eight
                         or nine hours' worth. Enough to
                         make it halfway to LA and back
                         if you had a mind to.

She thinks about it.

                                   DEBORAH
                         As a matter of fact I did drive
                         a fair way. I traveled down the
                         Peninsular to watch the sun rise
                         over the ocean.

                                   NASH
                         All on your own in peaceful
                         solitude.

                                   DEBORAH
                         Why, yes. Don't you believe me?

                                   NASH
                         It isn't a question of belief,
                         Mrs Dow. We have to make sense
                         of this. So let me put it this
                         way. As far as I'm concerned a
                         person's morals are their own
                         business - - if you follow - -

Deborah blankly shakes her head.

                                   NASH
                         All right. Laying it on the
                         line, it looks for all the
                         world as if you might have
                         been away seeing someone.

                                   DEBORAH
                         You mean another man? - - I
                         haven't.

                                   NASH
                         Fine. But let's suppose for a
                         minute you have. Now I can see
                         how that might be embarrassing.
                         But it wouldn't be the end of
                         the world. You might not believe
                         it, but we can be pretty discreet
                         about such things.
                              (pauses)
                         Well,Mrs Dow?

Deborah glares angrily at Nash, shaking her head.

                         DEBORAH
               This is horrible. I have been
               confronted with the most awful
               shock of my life - - my husband
               murdered. And you accuse me of - -

She seems about to burst into tears. But instead of tears, Deborah suddenly
sits upright, her mouth set with determination.

                         DEBORAH
               If this is to continue, I shall
               have to insist on calling my
               lawyer.

                         NASH
               You don't need a lawyer, Mrs Dow.
               You just need give a convincing
               account of your whereabouts.

Deborah makes no reply, staring straight ahead. Nash studies her, his
features hardening.

                         NASH
               You'll need to change your
               clothes.

                         DEBORAH
                  (confused, staring at
                  him)
               My clothes - - ?

                         NASH
               See it as a process of elimination.
               Your husband's remains will also
               have to be identified.

                         DEBORAH
               You mean - - ? But if he is as
               you say - -

                         NASH
               No, he's not a pretty sight. An
               ID is still required - - sorry.

He indicates to a young African-American woman officer standing close by.

                         NASH
               This officer will go with you,
               all right?

Deborah at first resists. She then quickly stands, and ignoring Nash, walks
numbly in the direction of the staircase.

Nash stalls the woman officer as she moves to follow.

                         NASH
               Make sure you get all her
               stuff. You understand?

The officer nods and goes after Deborah.

INT. KLEIN'S OFFICE - LATER

Klein, Gleeson and Nash are present, all three standing. Klein is in full
flow and angry:

                    KLEIN
          - - no justification for this.
          It flies in the face of all
          proper conduct.

                    GLEESON
          Is this really necessary, Nash?

                    NASH
          I know what I'm doing.

                    KLEIN
          And what precisely is that?
          What is it you hope to achieve?

                    GLEESON
          Yeah, I'm kind of scratching so
          far as that goes. We're dealing
          with influential people here.

                    NASH
          Don't give me that. She was
          with her lover, you know it
          and I know it.

                    KLEIN
          Even if you are right it doesn't
          follow they were implicated in
          murder.

                    GLEESON
          That's right.

                    NASH
          Look, I want to see her reaction,
          okay? And I want her stuff checked
          out.

                    KLEIN
          Stuff?

                    NASH
          Her clothes - - panties. Do I
          have to spell it out?

Klein gapes speechless as Gleeson fumbles. Nash checks his watch.

                    NASH
          Let's not keep the lady waiting

Klein looks to Gleeson, who looks down at his shoes. Klein shakes his head
then makes for the door, halting to turn back glaring at Nash.

                    KLEIN
          Incidentally, Creighton Dow's
          anal sphincter was ruptured.   (CONT'D)

                              Though what that gives you in
                              the light of all this I wouldn't
                              know.
                                   (exits)

INT. SMALL FUNCTIONAL WAITING ROOM

Deborah sits head lowered. She now wears dark slacks and a navy roll-neck
jumper and looks very pale and tense. The woman officer who collected her
clothes stands silently alongside.

Klein enters, Nash and Gleeson at his rear. Deborah comes anxiously to her
feet.

                                   DEBORAH
                              Can we get this over with?

Klein steps forward to lay a calming hand to her arm.

                                   KLEIN
                              I'm Doctor Klein, Mrs Dow.
                              This shouldn't take long.

Deborah allows him to lead her through plastic swing doors to:

INT. WHITE-TILED ROOM

Fluorescent tubes shed a hard bright light. The echoing space is empty save
for a single wheeled carriage covered by a MOUNDED WHITE SHEET.

Deborah stalls, her eyes fixing on the carriage. Klein leads her gently
forward. Nash sidles around to focus on Deborah.

                                   KLEIN
                              Don't be alarmed, Mrs Dow. An
                              actual sighting would be quite
                              pointless.

Deborah stares at him, confused.

                                   KLEIN
                              There must be some way to
                              substantiate that this is
                              your husband.
                                   (helping her
                                    along)
                              Some distinguishing mark,
                              perhaps?

Nash moves closer, his eyes narrowing.

                                   DEBORAH
                              Why, yes, a birthmark - -
                                   (trailing a
                                    finger)
                              About three inches long - -
                              running down from his neck.

Klein pats her arm and smiles.

                              KLEIN
                    There is such a mark.

Deborah sags with relief. Klein smiles and glances cunningly at Nash.

                              KLEIN
                    That would appear to satisfy
                    the matter.

He nods to an assistant, who steps forward to remove the carriage.

Nash takes Deborah by the arm and steers her forward. She reacts with
fear, eyes fixing on the mounded body. Nash reaches for the covering sheet.
Deborah braces back in horror. Nash studies her face for a second then lets
the sheet drop.

                              NASH
                    All right.

Nash lets go of her arm. Klein holds her around the shoulder and leads her
away. The room clears, leaving only Nash and Gleeson, who stares at Klein
with incomprehension.

                                        DISSOLVE TO:

INT. COFFEE SHOP - DAY

CHITA sits alone in a booth. About 40, her hair is cut short but with a
wave near covering one eye and dyed a garish yellow. Tattoos can be seen on
her bare arms and she is dressed in a flashy common manner, with perhaps a
very short leather skirt and high boots.

A sign reads NO SMOKING but she is nevertheless smoking with nervous
abandon. A supervisor approaches to reprimand her, but changes her mind and
settles for a testy look.

Fix on Chita's studied face, as DISSOLVE TO:

EXT. THE PAVILION AS SEEN IN DISTANCE THROUGH HIGH WINDOW - NIGHT

Chita stares out from her bedroom, drawing back instinctively, as from her
viewpoint a NAKED FIGURE hustles forward, too far away to be distinct.

INT. CHITA'S BEDROOM

She twists around in panic, knocking over a chair and bottles from off her
dressing table. She runs for the door.

INT. BANNISTERED CORRIDOR OVERLOOKING VAST GROUND-FLOOR ROOM

At the far end of the Room, as seen from Chita's viewpoint, French doors
crash open.

Chita swirls in panic. She wears a white shift, which she suddenly strips
off and dashes in her underwear to:

FIRE ESCAPE DOOR

Chita yanks at the bar handle, panicking as the Door stays locked,
shouting, "Come on - Come on - !" Seeing then that the Door is bolted top
and bottom, she snaps back the bolts, yanks the handle and goes out to:

                                                                    17

FIRE ESCAPE

Chita' descends in panic, worming through slats, squealing as she hurts her ribs, finally hanging to drop from the last platform. She rolls under the Fire Escape and huddles there. Across an expanse of lawn, from her viewpoint see a dense surround of trees and bushes.

A WHITE OBJECT floats into view and settles on the ground in front of her. Chita stares, seeing her white shift.

She then gives a sudden jump as a CRASH sounds from above.

Beneath Chita a pool of water spreads as she pees herself.

Chita hunches forward, one knee raised. She stalls, gasping air. And then she is running full pelt for the trees, as DISSOLVE BACK TO:

INT. COFFEE SHOP

Chita comes back to the moment. She stubs out the cigarette in a saucer and takes out a cell phone. She stares at the phone. Then making up her mind, she abruptly leaves the coffee shop.

                                                        DISSOLVE TO:

EXT. RITZ-CARLTON HOTEL - DAY - AS VIEWED FROM NASH'S PARKED CAR

Deborah and Veronica emerge and continue down steps to the car port.

Deborah wears a smart casual outfit, perhaps a blouse shirt and tailored camel slacks. Veronica, by contrast, is decked out in an outrageously short white dress and a giant pair of Ray-Bans covers a lot of her face. Both women appear aloof, not exchanging a word.

A bellman follows behind carrying an overnight case. A uniformed attendant holds open the door of Deborah's sportcar in readiness for their departure. The hood of the car is down. The bellman stows the case in the trunk. Deborah smiles at him by way of thanks and swings in behind the wheel.

Veronica meantime has settled in the passenger seat. The uniform closes Deborah's door. She kicks the engine into life, glances briefly at Veronica, and moves the car forward.

Nash watches as they drive away.

SERIES OF MERGING SHOTS TRACKING THE CAR'S JOURNEY:

        1. STREETS OF SAN FRANCICO
        2. SOUTHERN FREEWAY AND RIM OF GOLDEN GATE PARK
        3. GOLDEN GATE BRIDGE

INT OF CAR - DEBORAH AND VERONICA

The two women remain stiffly silent. Veronica lights a cigarette, tossing the spent match out into the wind.

                        VERONICA
                I'm still trying to figure this
                out. Here we are heading back to
                the old homestead for tea and
                sympathy. All the while getting   (CONT'D)

                                                                18

                    set to scratch each other's eyes
                    out over Creighton's loot.

Deborah shakes her head, concentrating on the road.

                         DEBORAH
                    I hope that isn't true.

                         VERONICA
                    It's true done up in pink ribbons.
                    How else can it be?

                         DEBORAH
                    It can be anyway we want. I hadn't
                    intended raising the question of
                    Creighton's will - -

                         VERONICA
                    But since I have - -

                         DEBORAH
                    Very well, since you have - -
                         (beat)
                    Suppose I told you I was prepared
                    to divide everything down the
                    middle.

Veronica turns and stares at her from behind the dark glasses.

                         VERONICA
                    You know something I don't?

                         DEBORAH
                    No hidden codicils, if that's what
                    you mean.

Veronica sits back and calmly smokes her cigarette.

                         VERONICA
                    You're a pretty cool customer,
                    aren't you? Creighton dead less
                    than twenty-four hours and already
                    down to the bone talking hard cash.

                         DEBORAH
                       (quickly)
                    I didn't mean to sound mercenary.
                    I simply wanted to avoid any
                    unpleasantness.

                         VERONICA
                    For sure, let's avoid any unpleasantness.
                       (draws on her
                       cigarette)
                    You certain that's how you want to
                    deal? A fifty-fifty split?

                         DEBORAH
                    The estate is set to be huge.
                    Why be greedy?

                        VERONICA
          Why indeed. Okay, so how do we
          move on it?

                        DEBORAH
          There is first the matter of the
          funeral - -

                        VERONICA
          I'll send a wreath. Stay with
          the will.

                        DEBORAH
             (after a pause)
          I had thought a pro tem agreement.

                        VERONICA
          Like a binding contract we both
          sign up for?

                        DEBORAH
          If you are agreeable. In fact I
          was going to suggest having dinner
          with my lawyer, Norman Pargeter,
          this evening.

                        VERONICA
          You don't waste time, do you?

                        DEBORAH
          Norman will be entirely impartial
          I assure you. He is a great fan
          of yours. He has seen lots of
          your films.

                        VERONICA
          Must be a masochist. Okay, why
          not? I've had an offer, of sorts.
          Over in Amsterdam. So the sooner
          we can wrap this up and I can be
          on my way is fine by me.

                        DEBORAH
          I thought you had done with all
          of that.

                        VERONICA
          Yeah, well, things don't always
          turn out the way you plan 'em. I
          tried the marriage bit, in case
          you forgot.

                        DEBORAH
          Yes, I'm sorry it didn't work out.

Veronica smiles sourly.

                        VERONICA
          He was con-artist. Fat, bald, and
          stony broke into the bargain - -

She stops in mid-track as Deborah stiffens.

                    VERONICA
               What's wrong?

Deborah squints angrily into her rear-view mirror.

REAR-VIEW MIRROR - WITH CAR FOLLOWING

                    DEBORAH
               Damn him!

Veronica twists to glance back.

                    VERONICA
               We got a tail? The press?

                    DEBORAH
               Hardly. My very own detective
               watchdog.

                    VERONICA
               A cop?

                    DEBORAH
               The man is nothing less than a
               sadist.

                    VERONICA
               Gave you a rough ride, did he?

                    DEBORAH
               I think you might call identifying
               Creighton's remains a rough ride.

Veronica smiles, tongue in cheek.

                    VERONICA
               Pull over. Let's take a look at
               this varmint.

Deborah holds a steady course for a while. She then decisively swings the
steering wheel.

EXT. FREEWAY

Deborah maneuvers through the traffic and brings her car to a halt on the
emergency lane. A car follows and parks fifteen feet or so behind. Nash
gets out and walks up to Deborah.

                    NASH
               You shouldn't stop here, Mrs Dow.

                    DEBORAH
               Have I broken some by-law?
                 (to Veronica)
               Allow me to introduce Inspector
               Nash, an extraordinary clever
               public servant.

Nash nods to Veronica, who removes her Ray-bans to look Nash over.

                    DEBORAH
          Why he is so clever he already
          knows the guilty party. Isn't
          that so, Inspector?
               (a beat)
          Oh, this is my sister-in-law.
          Who I am certain would be most
          interested to hear your views
          on the subject.

                    NASH
               (to Veronica)
          I've been wanting to meet you.

                    VERONICA
          Well here I am, kind sir. Free
          and available. Is that right,
          you know who done it?

                    DEBORAH
          Apparently, I am the monster. I
          lured my husband into the night
          and struck him down without a
          second thought.

                    NASH
          Nobody's saying that, Mrs Dow.

                    DEBORAH
          Really? I was under the impression
          I was as good as booked, judged,
          and sentenced.

                    NASH
          You know that isn't the case.
          But you must also know we have
          to follow any line that doesn't
          look right.

                    DEBORAH
          Meaning what, exactly?

Nash sees he is getting in too deep and makes to back off.

                    NASH
          Sorry for the intrusion. I'll
          let you continue your journey.

                    DEBORAH
               (making him halt)
          If you have anything to say then
          say it.

Nash tussles with good sense but gives in, coming back to the car.

                    NASH
          Okay, as I see it, there's a
          gap in your account that needs
          some urgent explaining.

Deborah and Nash lock eyes in mutual challenge, as at that moment a CRUISER draws to a halt behind Nash's car.

Nash glances back at the Cruiser then at Veronica.

                    NASH
          Could we talk?

                    VERONICA
          Oh, please. It seems I'll be
          staying with dear Deborah for
          a while. Why not give me a call,
          to steal a line? But then why
          wait?
               (holds out her
               fisted hands)
          You can take me in now.

Nash smiles a flinty smile and again glances back at the Cruiser. A patrol cop in shirtsleeves has stepped out and moves in a measured way toward Deborah's car.

                    NASH
          You'll need to drive on,
          Mrs Dow.

He nods again to Veronica and walks toward the patrol officer. They are joined by a second younger officer. Nash shows his badge and they wait.

Then Deborah starts the car and re-joins the freeway, Nash and the two officers watching as she picks up speed.

INT. MAIN ROOM OF THE DOW MANSION - LATER

Deborah leads ahead of Veronica to the heart of the room.

                    DEBORAH
          Help yourself to a drink, I
          have to make a call.
               (turns away)

                    VERONICA
               (glancing around)
          To your lawyer? Sure you want
          to? Nash looked the real deal
          to me.

Deborah pauses, shakes her head.

                    DEBORAH
          I simply am not prepared to
          tolerate his bullying tactics
          a moment longer.

                    VERONICA
          Yeah? Seems to me you might
          have done some promoting of
          the exchange.

                    DEBORAH
          That is ridiculous.

                    VERONICA
          If you say so. I take it you
          do want to see Creighton's
          killer rounded up?

                    DEBORAH
          Certainly I do.

                    VERONICA
          Then could be Nash is your man.
          All right, so he ruffled your
          feathers. But this is no picnic
          and might be he's got a point.
          He laid it on the line, and I
          like that.

Deborah pauses as she deliberates.

                    DEBORAH
          We'll see.
               (strides away)

INT. THE MASTER BEDROOM - A MOMENT LATER

The room is impressively grand, tall double windows draped in chintz, with
a large rounded double bed in evidence.

Deborah goes directly to the bedside telephone. She hesitates then lifts
the phone and dials. The connexion is made, there is a pause and she then
speaks intently.

                    DEBORAH
          We have a problem - -

OIL PAINTING OF ZACHARY DOW

Veronica stands staring up at the Painting, her face grim.

Deborah reappears. She pauses then moves up to stand beside Veronica
silently sharing her upward view. Veronica sees that Deborah as joined her.

                    VERONICA
          So the old bastard's still king
          of the walk.

                    DEBORAH
          Creighton never could bring
          himself to have it removed.
               (breaks position)
          What about that drink?

                    VERONICA
          First I'd like to go to the
          pavilion.

Deborah stiffens.

                    DEBORAH
          There really isn't anything to
          see.

                                                                    24

                              VERONICA
                    I still would like to take a
                    look - - if you don't mind.

Left without choice, Deborah nods and leads on through French Doors.

PAVILION

They come to a halt and stand side by side about ten feet back from the
Pavilion Doors.

                              DEBORAH
                    As I understand, he was lying
                    here.

They both gaze down in morose silence. Veronica's face is pinched. Deborah
shrewdly watches along the line of her eyes.

Then in one sudden movement Veronica goes down on her knees and reaches to
run a flatted hand over the death spot.

                                                    DISSOLVE TO:

INT. SAN FRANCISCO BAR/RESTAURANT - EVENING

GRANT BOWMAN and TERRY sit facing one another in a booth. Terry is about
28, fair and pretty. Grant is a big powerful man, about 35, and good-
looking in a brutish sort of way.

They have drinks in front of them, beer for Grant, who is grinning and
coming on strong to Terry, who looks decidedly uneasy. She glances up
seeing Nash and manages a relieved smile. Nash joins them, frowning.

                              NASH
                        (to Terry)
                    Sorry I'm late.

                              TERRY
                        (nodding to Grant)
                    This is - -

Grant cuts in, grinning broadly. He is here made to speak with an
Australian accent, but with a few dialogue shifts can as easily be made a
Texan or suchlike. The idea is to present him as a menacing character with
rough, unconventional speech patterns.

                              GRANT
                        (pushing out a
                        big paw)
                    Grant Bowman, to give the full
                    monika. You'd be Nash, right?

Nash nods and warily shakes hands.

                              GRANT
                    I was told I might find you
                    here.
                        (grins at Terry)
                    No sweat, of course. Terry makes
                    waiting a real pleasure. Take a
                    pew, why don't ya.

Terry sidles out from the Booth.

>   TERRY
>   Need to freshen up - - back
>   in a sec.

As she eases past Nash she rolls her eyes and walks off to find the rest
rooms. Grant watches her departure with unconcealed lechery.

>   GRANT
>   Nice pert little bum on her,
>   ain't she?
>   (to Nash)
>   You're a lucky bloke.

Nash sits and waits for Grant to speak.

>   GRANT
>   What do you weigh?

>   NASH
>   What do I weigh?

>   GRANT
>   Yeah, what's your weight class?
>   - - middle, light-heavy - - ?

>   Nash
>   Is that important?

>   GRANT
>   Might be, you never know. I'd
>   take a stab at one-eighty - -
>   yeah, about that I'd say. I could
>   give you twenty pounds, easy.

>   NASH
>   There's a thought.

>   GRANT
>   One to toy with. (grins)Don't
>   You want to know who I am?

>   NASH
>   You just told me.

>   GRANT
>   I mean - -

>   NASH
>   I know what you mean. You're on
>   the team. You're a cop, right?
>   Thought I'd seen you before.

>   GRANT.
>   Not bad, sport. Like they say,
>   takes one to know one. And could
>   be our paths did cross some time.
>   Not for a while, though. They
>   shipped me out to Valley to put
>   roses in my cheeks.

                    NASH
          You don't tell me?

                    GRANT
          Yeah, twee upper-class Mill
          Valley. It's a healthy life
          if a touch dull at times.

                    NASH
          So is that why you're here, to
          run over the benefits of your
          out-of-town posting?

                    GRANT
          You know better than that. No,
          thought it was time you and me
          had a little chinwag.

                    NASH
          Oh, yeah?

                    GRANT
          Yeah - - seeing we're up to our
          necks in the same razzmatazz
          case. Brothers in arms, as you
          might say. Though beats me why
          it was deemed useful to call you
          to the colors.

                    NASH
          It's a mystery, all right.

                    GRANT
          You reckon? Nah, they shit bricks
          having this big murder doings drop
          in their lap. Stupid when yours'
          truly could have handled it.

                    NASH
          Why didn't you?

                    GRANT
          Not my call, was it? I've sorta
          come into things later, you know
          doin' a bit of tidying up. Which
          is why I'm here now. To offer
          some advice.

                    NASH
          Okay, I'm listening.

                    GRANT
            (eyes narrowing)
          You'd be sensible to do that,
          sport. I mean, high-flyer like
          yourself. Top notch lifestyle,
          birds galore. Why put that in
          jeopardy?

                    NASH
          Is that what I'm doing?

                    GRANT
          Could just be. Could be you're
          in danger of becoming a pain
          up the rectum, and we wouldn't
          want that, now would we?

                    NASH
          I guess not.

                    GRANT
          Right can lead to problems,
          if you're not careful.

Grant stares with hard meaning. Terry comes back, halting reading the
situation. Grant looks up at her and grins.

                    GRANT
          Ah, here she is. That was
          quick. Nice though. Musky.
          I can smell you from here.

Terry doesn't know whether to laugh this off. Grant stands and gazes down
intently at Nash.

                    GRANT
          We could get on real well,
          you and me, sport. All a
          question of seein' the other
          bloke's point of view. Just
          need to play the game, know
          what I mean?

He winks, knocks back his beer, then digs out some bills and tosses them on
the table.

                    GRANT
          Have a round on me. G'night.

He leers at Terry and walks away. She sits and frowns at Nash.

                    TERRY
          What was that all about?

Nash picks up a bill and smiles ruefully.

                    NASH
          I've just been warned off.

                                        DISSOLVE TO:

EXT. FISHERMAN'S WHARF - EVENING

Deborah and Veronica sit either side of NORMAN PARGETER in the terrace of a
chic restaurant. The weather is balmy and people move around lazily,
tourists, lovers hand in hand, etc, the Bay and the Golden Gate Bridge
forming a perfect backdrop.

Pargeter and Veronica are both smoking. Pargeter is in his early forties,
smoothly good-looking and dressed with casual expensive effect. He is in
full flow as the scene opens.

                    PARGETER
          - - the cinema has held a
          fascination for me since my
          halcyon college days.

                    VERONICA
          You are a buff.

                    PARGETER
          Yes, I think that designation
          would serve. And now I am in
          heaven. To be actually dining
          with a star of the silver screen.

                    VERONICA
          A somewhat tarnished star, I fancy.

                    PARGETER
          Nonsense. Yours was - - is a
          a sublime art.

                    VERONICA
          Want a job as my press agent?
             (takes a drink)
          I hear you have caught some of
          my stuff.

                    PARGETER
          Indeed I have.
             (kisses his
             fingertips)
          Wonderful!

                    VERONICA
          Sublime - - wonderful. This gets
          better.

                    DEBORAH
             (cutting in)
          Veronica is thinking about
          resuming her career, Norman.
          Isn't that so, Veronica - -
          a film offer in Amsterdam?

                    VERONICA
          About it, my big comeback.

                    PARGETER
          This is truly good news. Needless
          to say, I await the release with
          rapt anticipation.

                    VERONICA
          I'll try not to disappoint. But
          I'm interested in these Oscar
          pedigree vehicles of mine you
          found so enthralling.

Pargeter smiles and swills brandy around the bowl of his glass, glancing
to Deborah.

                    PARGETER
          Veronica doesn't think I'm trading
          square. She thinks I'm fibbing.
               (to Veronica)
          Are you in a sporting mood?

                    VERONICA
          I dunno. What's the bet?

                    PARGETER
          That to your satisfaction I can
          describe the plots and characters
          of your key works - - for a suitable
          reward, of course.

Veronica smiles and nods.

                    VERONICA
          Okay, describe away.

                    PARGETER
          Excellent - -
               (gazes into space)
          The two I would cite above all
          would be *Heat Death* and *Salem
          Blood Legacy* - - oh, and of
          course *Robo Fiend Girl*, which
          I hold to be truly special.

                    VERONICA
               (tipping her head)
          You win a cigar.

Pargeter toasts her with his brandy, pleased with himself.

                    PARGETER
          I have relished all those films,
          and more.

                    VERONICA
          And you saw *Robo Fiend Girl*?
          Which so happens to have been
          my swan song.

                    PARGETER
          Only your latest to date. Now
          what of my reward? I had hoped
          for a little more than a cigar.

Veronica smiles an enigmatic smile.

                    VERONICA
          I'll think of something.
               (shifts her chair)
          Think I'll take the air. Deborah,
          I know, is eager to discuss a
          certain pressing matter.

                    PARGETER
          You are referring to this troublesome
          Nash fellow.

                    DEBORAH
          Veronica believes I am over-reacting,
          Norman. She thinks I should allow
          him to continue his investigation.

                    PARGETER
          That would of course be the easier
          option. It rather depends on how
          strongly you feel his behaviour has - -

Veronica leaves them to it and strolls to the rail of Pier 41 and gazes
pensively in the direction of Alcatraz and Sausalito.

She turns to the crowded walkways of Fisherman's Wharf.

HUBUB OF NOISE, which drains to:

DEAD SILENCE

Veronica stares into crowd to see what might be:

OBSCURE FACE PEERING BACK

FADE TO BLACK

INT. SHABBY HOTEL ROOM - DAY

Chita sits on a cot bed in her underwear, a phone tight to her head.

Hear RINGING ON THE LINE, which stops as the connexion is made.

Chita waits, her stress evident. Then hear Creighton Dow's effeminate
voice:

                    CREIGHTON (V.O.)
          Well, sweetie, in your own time - -

Chita reacts, punching the air. She then blurts:

                    CHITA
          Wanna guess who this is!

Hear Creighton chuckle.

                    CREIGHTON (V.O.)
          Chita. You have called at last.

                    CHITA
          You - you bet I called - an' an'
          you know what I want - an' an
          lot's more on top - -

                    CREIGHTON (V.O.)
          Calm yourself, Chita. Your
          dividend was never in dispute.

                    CHITA
          You bastard! You think I'm dumb
          or somethin'! You was gettin' all
          set to rub me out!

                    CREIGHTON (V.O.)
          Chita, I swear - -

                    CHITA
          An' you almost got me! I near
          busted a couple of ribs on that
          fuckin' fire escape, you asshole!

                    CREIGHTON (V.O.)
          I am indeed sorry it has come to
          this.

                    CHITA
          Yeah, well you're gonna be a
          whole lot sorrier when I get
          through with you!

In her excitement, the phone slips from Chita's fingers and she scrabbles
to retrieve it.

                    CHITA
          You still there? You ain't
          gone away?

                    CREIGHTON (V.O.)
             (with weary
             sarcasm)
          No, I *ain't* gone away.

                    CHITA
          Right, good, I bin figurin'.
          We gotta meet - - today. An'
          no funny business - -

                    CREIGHTON (V.O.)
          Nothing was further from my mind.

                    CHITA
          - - Know why? 'Cause I got the
          right shit held with a certain
          somebody - - Geddit!

                    CREIGHTON (V.O.)
          Chita, that is so corny.

                    CHITA
          Yeah, sure it is. But you know
          what, it works. Try any smart
          stuff an' the whole fuckin'
          shebang gets blown!

                    CREIGHTON (V.O.)
          Then let us talk, as you suggest.

                    CHITA
          We'll skip the talk. Just bring
          fifty grand, got it!

                    CREIGHTON (V.O.)
          A mere fifty thousand? I could
          easily double that.

                                                            32

                    CHITA
               (flustered)
          I told you not to start gettin'
          cute.

                    CREIGHTON (V.O.)
          This is straight goods. Think
          of it. A nice crisp one hundred
          thousand dollars in your hand.
          It so happens I have such a tidy
          sum all ready and waiting. There
          may even be a bonus.

                    CHITA
          Wha-what you mean?

                    CREIGHTON
          Extras. I have a job for you.

Chita gazes fitfully about her, suspecting a trap.

                    CHITA
          What job you talkin' about?

                    CREIGHTON (V.O.)
          One you are very well-suited to
          perform. It concerns my dear
          wayward wife. Also my equally
          dear little sister. Who has
          returned temporarily to the
          fold.

Chita becomes highly alarmed, eyes darting as if seeking an escape.

                    CHITA
               (finding her
               voice)
          What kind of crazy world you
          live - - ?

                    CREIGHTON (V.O.)
          Now, I take it you have a
          rendezvous worked out.

                    CHITA
          Don't forget I got insurance.

                    CREIGHTON (V.O.)
          I won't. But remember, Chita.
          In scuppering me you scupper
          yourself.
               (beat)
          So where and when, darling - -

Chita swallows and goes for it.

                    CHITA
          You know Grace Cathedral?

                    CREIGHTON (V.O.)
          Good choice.

                         CHITA
              Be there at five.

                         CREIGHTON (V.O.)
              Grace Cathedral - - five this
              evening it is.

                         CHITA
              An' don't forget the dough.

                         CREIGHTON (V.O.)
              It will be there - - Oh, should
              you arrive first - -

                         CHITA
              Yeah? What?

                         CREIGHTON (V.O.)
              Say a quick one for me - -

INT. CAR TRAVELLING THROUGH SAN FRANCISCO - DAY

Nash and BRIAN CONNOR being chauffeured through the city. Connor is Nash's
boss, a wiry intelligent man in his early fifties. Neither he nor Nash look
happy, avoiding eye contact.

                         CONNOR
              You had to have it your way.

They travel on in silence.

                         NASH
              She's mixed up in it, Brian.
              I know she is.

Connor makes no comment.

                         NASH
              Her story doesn't add up.

                         CONNOR
              Maybe, but right now we can't
              show much by way of back-up.

They travel on, both gazing morosely out at the passing city.

                         NASH
              So now we have to go cap in hand
              to Pargeter's office like a
              couple of naughty schoolkids.

                         CONNER
              I don't like it any more than
              you do. But you played this
              too strong, Dick.

                         NASH
              I might have been a tad rough
              on her.

                    CONNOR
          Halleluiah! Dick Nash admits he
          he just might have over-stepped
          the mark. She'll be there this
          morning, don't forget. Won't
          hurt to think about offering
          an apology.

                    NASH
          Jesus.

                    CONNOR
          See it as an exercise in self-
          discipline. Keep any smart-aleck
          comebacks under your hat. Don't,
          whatever you do, let that slick
          shyster get under your skin.

Nash grunts. Connor gives him a dubious look, as DISSOLVE TO:

INT. VERONICA'S BEDROOM - FROM ANGLE OF GAPED DOOR - DAY

Veronica comes out from the bathroom towelling off. She glances at the bed,
where her open valise and clothes are laid out.

From the viewpoint of the Gaped Door, Veronica, in black underwear, begins
to dress, squeezing into a black catsuit. She manages to zip herself up and
sits on the bed facing a cheval mirror, and lost in thought she begins to
comb out her wet hair.

Checking in the mirror she then sees REFLECTION OF BLURRED FIGURE.

The figure sharpens into focus, as we see Grant leering.

INT. VERONICA'S BEDROOM

Veronica comes twisting to her feet. Too late to duck back, Grant grins his
confident grin and steps into the room.

                    GRANT
          Lo there.

Veronica gapes at him, unable to speak. Grant strolls on further into the
room, freely looking her over.

                    GRANT
          Sure fits nice and snug, that
          outfit.

                    VERONICA
             (finding her
             voice)
          Who are you? What are you doing
          here?

                    GRANT
          Just my duty. I'm the law, see.

                    VERONICA
          You mean you're a policeman?

                    GRANT
One of the brave boys in blue
- - Detective Bowman. But you
can call me Grant.

                    VERONICA
And - and your duties extend to
spying into guest's bedrooms?

                    GRANT
Being of service is how I see it.
Makin' sure you good ladies are
tucked up safe and sound.

                    VERONICA
Service, is that what you call it?

                    GRANT
Sure, real serviceable bloke,
that's me. Could be of service
to you, lady all on her own.
You're the sister, am I right?
Used to be in pictures. Real
sorry about your brov.

                    VERONICA
You knew him?

                    GRANT
Got on with him a treat. Shame
what happened. Still, you're   .
here, that's what counts.

                    VERONICA
Is it?

                    GRANT
Absolutely. Life's for the
living, right? - - I saw one
of your flicks one time.

                    VERONICA
Oh?

                    GRANT
Yeah, set in the Everglades or
some such. You was running through
this burning swamp in your smalls
and there was this scary monster
freak comin' right there after you.
I reckon I could see what he had
in mind. You had yeller hair then
and it was a lot longer. Suited me
better than like you got it now.

                    VERONICA
Did it?

                    GRANT
You bet. I like a woman to look
like a woman.

Veronica turns nervily and busies herself packing things away.

> VERONICA
> Interesting though all this is,
> we'll have to save it for some
> other time.

> GRANT
> Set to be leavin'?

> VERONICA
> (tossing the comb
> into the valise)
> That's the plan.

Grant moves up behind her.

> GRANT
> Seems a pity.

He lifts a wet strand of Veronica's hair and sets it carefully in place.
She holds still, flinching as his big hand lingers to touch damply at the
nape of her neck.

> GRANT
> You are one sexy lady, you
> know that.

Veronica shifts position, becoming breathless.

> VERONICA
> I suppose that's meant as a
> compliment.

> GRANT
> Sure it's a compliment. I got
> the gift. Ladies have paid
> good money for my attention.

> VERONICA
> (trying to joke)
> With references to prove it,
> no doubt.

Saying this, Veronica makes to move clear. Grant suddenly wraps his arms
around her from behind, pinning her tight.

Veronica stands shocked, unable to move. Grant nuzzles her neck, and
holding her in place, his free clamps her breast. Veronica stands paralyzed
as his hand roams to stroke at her abdomen. She sways and seems about to
faint. And then she is shouting:

> VERONICA
> Get off me, you motherfucker!

> GRANT
> Asking for it rough?

> VERONICA
> I'm not asking for it any way!
> Get away from me! Do you hear!

Grant's face is ragged with lust, his urge to rape in the balance.

Then his grip slackens. Veronica stumbles from him, gasping for air. Grant backs away, grinning.

                              GRANT
                    No offence took, I hope. Little
                    bit of pattacake is all.

Veronica leans hunched over the bed, head bowed as though fighting nausea.

                              VERONICA
                    Just get out!

Grant exits grinning. Veronica tumbles across the room and slams the door shut behind him. Then cradles her head and pounds a fist weakly at the door and begins to weep.

INT. NORMAN PARGETER'S OFFICE

Pargeter looks up from behind a handsome exec desk as Nash and Connor enter. He is dressed to the nines in a pinstripe dark suit and sports black horn-rimmed glasses as if to stress his domination.

Across the room Deborah stands gazing absently through a Georgian window, with maybe Coit Tower visible in the distance. She is immaculately dressed in a silver two-piece suit and displays a minimum of jewellery.

Pargeter nods at two strategically placed chairs. He does not rise or offer his hand. Connor sits as directed. Nash remains standing. Pargeter swivels his chair to face Deborah.

                              PARGETER
                    When you are ready, Deborah.

Deborah nods and walks with a mysterious smile on her lips to seat herself in a leather chair to Pargeter's right. She demurely crosses her legs and tugs the hem of her skirt in place above her knee.

Nash focuses on her knees. She catches him looking and gives the skirt a further tug. Pargeter amusedly notices this.

                              PARGETER
                    Do you think you might sit,
                    Inspector? We won't be making
                    a charge.

Nash glances at his chair and sits. Pargeter smiles faintly in approval then constructs a grave demeanor.

                              PARGETER
                    Coming directly to the matter
                    at hand, my client feels she
                    has grounds for serious complaint
                    against Inspector Nash.

Turning to Deborah, he indicates toward Connor.

                              PARGETER
                    I should introduce Captain Connor.

Deborah and Connor exchange nods of greeting.

                    CONNOR
          Naturally, we are sorry if we
          have caused you upset, Mrs Dow.

                    PARGETER
          This is no trivial matter to
          be brushed aside with standard
          apologies, Captain.

                    CONNOR
          With all due respect, I was
          simply expressing my concern.
          I would point out that we are
          involved with a particularly
          difficult homicide and such
          investigations are never easy.

                    PARGETER
          That hardly excuses Inspector
          Nash's behaviour, which - - and
          I choose my words with care - -
          has bordered on the obsessive.

                    CONNOR
          Obsessive? I can't - -

                    PARGETER
          You doubt that? In the small hours
          of Sunday morning, following the
          tragic events we are all consumed
          with, he practically accused my
          client of being absent in the
          company of another man - - an
          outrageous suggestion.

                    NASH
          Then where the hell was she?

                    PARGETER
             (narrowing his
             gaze)
          Moderate your tone, if you
          please, Inspector. You are
          not meting out one of your
          third degree interviews.

                    CONNOR
             (muttering)
          Yes, Inspector, remember why
          we are here.

                    PARGETER
          Thank you, Captain. He then insisted
          she give up the clothes she was
          wearing - - *all* of her clothes.

                    NASH
          They were needed to clear her
          presence at the crime scene.

                    PARGETER
          So you suspected her?

                    NASH
          We have to cover all bases.

                    PARGETER
          Cover all bases? I see.
            (head shake)
          If all of this were not enough,
          he then compelled her to travel
          to the police mortuary where she
          was made to view her husband's
          remains. A young wife in a state
          of virtual shock.

                    CONNOR
          We sometimes have to do unpleasant
          things.

                    PARGETER
          So it would appear.
            (beat)
          Were you aware, Captain, that
          Inspector Nash forced Mrs Dow off
          the freeway yesterday afternoon?

Connor almost winces.

                    PARGETER
          Oh, yes, and where he again as
          good as accused her of being
          complicit in her husband's murder.

                    NASH
          No one forced Mrs Dow off the
          freeway and no accusation were
          made. I wanted to speak with
          her sister-in-law, that's all.

Pargeter shakes his head with phony disapproval.

                    PARGETER
          I am somewhat bemused and very
          disappointed.

                    NASH
          Is that right? Then think on
          this. Here we are, using up
          valuable police time sorting
          out Mrs Dow's injured feelings,
          when the core issue, the murder
          of her husband, gets lost in
          the shuffle.

Pargeter makes a weary sigh and turns to Deborah.

                    PARGETER
          It would appears we are left
          with no alternative other than
          press for Inspector Nash's removal.

Deborah, who has sat listening with eyes downcast, now raises her gaze.

                         DEBORAH
              I would prefer not to do that,
              Norman.

She turns and directs her gaze at Nash.

                         DEBORAH
              I understand Inspector Nash's
              position. Put simply he has not
              been able to fully satisfy himself
              of my innocence. Isn't that so,
              Inspector?

                         NASH
              I'm only trying to reach the
              truth.

                         CONNOR
              I am certain Inspector Nash
              bears no animosity toward you,
              Mrs Dow.

                         DEBORAH
              Yes, Captain, I think I do see
              that. And having now given the
              matter some thought, I believe
              I would be happy if he were
              allowed to continue with his
              investigations.

                         PARGETER
              Are you certain about this,
              Deborah?

                         DEBORAH
              I believe so, Norman.
                (to Connor)
              I take it you consider Inspector
              Nash to be a worthy officer,
              Captain?

                         CONNOR
              Nash is one of our very best
              detectives, Mrs Dow. I can vouch
              for that.

                         DEBORAH
              Then I see no problem.

She again directs her gaze at Nash, and a certain sexual chemistry is
generated between them.

                         DEBORAH
              It would of course be a rather
              nice gesture if he were to offer
              something of an apology for the
              distress he has caused me.

The room falls silent. Connor glances at Nash, urging him to say the right words. Pargeter sits preoccupied with a thumbnail. Deborah is smiling a faint smile. Nash gazes at her and returns his own crooked smile.

                    NASH
          All right, Mrs Dow, I'm sorry
          - - truly. I apologize, is
          that okay? But thanks for the
          vote of confidence. In return
          I'll do all I can to find the
          answer to this thing.

Their eyes lock.

                    DEBORAH
          I don't doubt it.

                                        DISSOLVE TO:

EXT. ESTABLISHING SHOT OF RITZ-CARLTON HOTEL - DUSK

INT. VERONICA'S HOTEL BEDROOM

She enters, clearly exhausted, going directly to flop fully-clothed on the bed where she plunges into immediate sleep, as DISSOLVE TO:

INT. GRACE CATHEDRAL

Chita wanders around the vast space, gazing up and around, at the high ceiling, the stained glass windows. Other visitors are in evidence, tourists and worshippers, possibly the odd nun and priest.

Chita's agitation is evident. She is nevertheless sassy enough to dip her finger into the holy water bowl and then kneel quickly and cross herself facing the altar, coming upright with a sardonic smile.

Glancing around, she wanders around the basilica and past the big main altar, nervousness mounting.

She then enters a colonnade aisle. Few people are in evidence. In a recess, she stares up at a statue of the Virgin Mary.

Chita freezes, her face suddenly etched in terror.

                                        DISSOLVE TO:

INT. VERONICA'S BEDROOM AT THE RIZ-CARLTON

Veronica returns woozily to consciousness. Muted traffic noise is heard from outside. The room is now in semi-darkness. She rises and plods unsteadily to stare into a smoked glass mirror, as CROSSFADE TO:

INT. VERONICA'S BEDROOM - HER REFLECTION IN THE MIRROR

Veronica holds a champagne glass. The room is now softly-lit and she is dressed in vampish fashion: silver fox curly wig, a short close-fitting dress of vermillion red, her lips are rouged and eyes heavily mascaraed.

TELEPHONE RINGS OUT

Veronica jolts staring at the Phone, then guardedly and lifts the instrument, and we hear Creighton's now familiar voice:

                         CREIGHTON (V.O.)
                I expect you are well on the way
                to ruin by now, Verro,

Veronica drops the glass, which bounces spilling champagne over the carpet.

We hear Creighton giggle, as if seeing this.

EXT. RITZ-CARLTON HOTEL - UPWARD VIEW FROM STREET - CONTINUOUS

From Creighton's p.o.v. in the shadows, only the darkened back of his head
and shoulders in evidence, see the lighted windows of the Hotel.

                         CREIGHTON (V.O.)
                So, have you missed me so terribly
                terribly? Silly question. Of course
                you have missed me, as I have you.
                But we shall be as one again soon.

INT. VERONICA'S HOTEL ROOM

She gapes, unable to speak, staring at her shocked reflection.

                         VERONICA
                No - -

                         CREIGHTON (V.O.)
                    (on the line)
                Could my ears have deceived me?
                Was that a 'no' I heard? Oh, dear.
                I see now the error of my ways. I
                took you for granted.

                         VERONICA
                Whoever you are, please leave me
                alone.

                         CREIGHTON (V.O.)
                Leave? Verro darling, you know
                full well I could never contemplate
                such a wanton act.

See as Veronica sees THE ROOM TILTING.

                         VERONICA
                But - - But - -

                         CREIGHTON (V.O.)
                Yes, what is it that troubles you?

                         VERONICA
                You - - you are dead - -

                         CREIGHTON (V.O.)
                    (tittering laugh)
                Not I. Very much close at hand,
                in fact.

                         VERONICA
                Wh -where are you?

                                                                    43

EXT. RITZ-CARLTON HOTEL - SHOOTING UP AS BEFORE

                    CREIGHTON (V.O.
               On the street where you live.

EXT. VERONICA'S HOTEL ROOM

She fumbles to the window and peers down at the street below.

                    CREIGHTON (V.O.)
                 (on the line)
               Shall I wave a handkerchief?
                 (laughs)
               To set your mind at rest. It is
               true, a corpse now resides tagged
               with my name. Happily it is not
               my corpse.

Veronica staggers away from the window.

                    VERONICA
               How - - how - - ?

                    CREIGHTON (V.O.)
               Ah, that would be telling. And to
               pre-empt your next question, I gave
               it twenty-four hours with darling
               Deborah before you skittered back
               to your Ritz bolt-hole. You may as
               well face it, Verro. I know you as
               I know myself. We have a bond - -
               sealed in blood, one might say.

                    VERONICA
               No - -

                    CREIGHTON (V.O.)
               Tut, tut, the best education that
               bad money can buy, and all you do
               is grunt words like some wretched
               fish peddler.

Veronica sways as if about to topple over.

EXT. RITZ-CARLTON HOTEL - UPWARD FROM CREIGHTON'S POV

                    CREIGHTON (V.O.)
               Verro? Hel-loo? Are you still
               with us?

INT. VERONICA'S HOTEL ROOM

                    VERONICA
               What is it you want?

                    CREIGHTON (V.O.)
                 (on the line)
               Excellent, a response - - What
               do I want? I want what is mine.
               Nothing more nor less. When we
               meet I shall explain all - -

                    VERONICA
          I don't want to see you!

                    CREIGHTON (V.O.)
          Now tomorrow you have this will-reading
          nonsense to broker- - what an avaricious
          pair you are. Are you curious to know
          how the pie slices? Well, Verro, you
          will find, hint, hint, that you have
          not come out half badly. So, after you
          and Deborah have bristled your tails
          at one another, make haste to our hidden
          theatre of sin. There is a good feature
          running so I am informed. One boasting a
          new *young* star. I shall be in my favourite
          seat. If you are good I may buy you a
          tuti-fruity ice cream.

                    VERONICA
          I - I have a flight to catch.

EXT. RITZ-CARLTON HOTEL - FROM CREIGHTON'S POV

                    CREIGHTON (V.O.)
          To Amsterdam, yes I know. When we have
          concluded by all means go, if that is
          what your heart yearns. I do fear,
          however, you are headed for a bitter
          disappointment.

INT. VERONICA'S HOTEL ROOM.

                    VERONICA
          It's a chance I must take.

                    CREIGHTON (V.O.)
               (on the line)
          There is no chance. In your last two
          or three outings it was as stark as
          graffiti on a lavatory wall that time's
          winged chariot had hurried by.

                    VERONICA
          You are cruel - - like Creighton.

                    CREIGHTON (V.O.)
          Nature is herself cruel, Verro, and
          the cruellest act is to play the false
          prophet. You had a certain brash sexuality
          which for a while we were able to exploit.
          Now that hour has passed.

                    VERONICA
               (weeping)
          I hate you.

                    CREIGHTON (V.O.)
          Yes, yes, you hate me. Verro, you
          are becoming a bore. Tomorrow, fix
          on that. You know where you have
          to go?

                    VERONICA
          I know.

                    CREIGHTON (V.O.)
          Good. Try not to be late. We are
          set to have some fun again.

                    VERONICA
          Dear God, no - -

EXT. RITZ-CARLTON HOTEL - UPWARD FROM CREIGHTON'S POV

                    CREIGHTON (V.O.)
          Since when did you ever believe
          in God - - ?

Creighton draws back into shadows - -

INT. VERONICA'S HOTEL ROOM

The phone drops limply and after a moment Veronica sinks to the carpet,
staring dead eyes at the blurred lights beyond the window.

CUT TO PHONE ON CARPET

A distant voice calls out, "Room Service - - hello, this is Room Service,
can we help - -?" as CROSSFADE TO BLACK:

INT. VERONICA'S BEDROOM AS SHE RETURNS TO LIFE

A DRILL sounds as if inside her head, which becomes the DOOR BUZZER.

Veronica stirs, blinking, and after a moment struggles giddily to her feet.
She staggers to the door, hesitating.

                    VERONICA
          Who - who is it?

Nash speaks from behind the door.

                    NASH (O.S.)
          Nash -- remember? The rude
          cop.

                    VERONICA
          Just a minute - -

She blunders to the mirror, makes a fast correcting job, and goes back and
opens the door.

Nash stands propped to the doorframe, reacting with surprise by Veronica's
appearance.

                    VERONICA
          Come on in, Inspector. Step
          into my parlor. Sorry to have
          kept you waiting.

Nash follows Veronica into her suite. His foot bumps the upturned champagne
glass and he stoops to retrieve it. She smiles and takes the glass.

                    VERONICA
          Clumsy. I was having myself a
          little snort - - and right now
          I need another. Champagne, do
          you go for it?

                    NASH
          When I can get it.

                    VERONICA
          Top of the range. No cheap
          fizz-water here.

She makes it to where a silver ice bucket and glasses are set out and
reaches out the started bottle, holding it up to the light to peer through
the thick green glass.

                    VERONICA
          Nearly all gone - - like life.
          The end comes all too fast.
               (beat)
          But why be morbid? We have
          more in reserve and the night
          is young.

She fills two glasses and sways unsteadily toward Nash, champagne spilling
and he moves fast to grab a glass. Veronica steadies her balance and raises
her glass.

                    VERONICA
          Well - - here's to crime. That's
          what they say in the old movies.
          Here's to crime, they say, but
          never in real life. It only gets
          to be said in the old black and
          white movies you catch when you
          can't sleep. Anyway, that corny
          stuff's all wrong for the occasion.
          Or is, Inspector?
               (screwing her eyes)
          In-spec-tor. Do I have to keep
          calling you that?

                    NASH
          Try Dick.

                    VERONICA
          Dick? Yeah, it suits you - -
          hits sharp. A touch of the rascal
          about it.

She set down her glass and moves closer.

                    VERONICA
          You are very attractive, Dick,
          you know that? Sure you do. All
          attractive men know it, damn them.
          Married too. Yeah, got little wifey
          waiting back at the ranch.

                    NASH
          Not last time I looked.

                    VERONICA
          Well - - how did you escape?
          Girlfriends though, I'll bet.

                    NASH
          No more than a dozen or so, in
          my little black book.

                    VERONICA
          You dog.
             (drains her glass)
          I'm a veteran of many campaigns,
          though in hock but once. It's
          a sad tale, Dick my friend, and
          I'm all used up with sad tales.

She snakes her free arm around Nash's neck to give him a fast soul kiss.
She pushes back.

                    VERONICA
          Call it a down-payment.
             (sad head-shake)
          But got to tell you - - Deborah's
          not here. Unless she's hiding
          under the bed. She's the one you
          are chasing down, am I right? That
          tough-guy routine you pulled was
          just so much hooey. You want to
          get into her pants, and don't tell
          me otherwise.

Veronica all at once becomes seriously anguished.

                    VERONICA
          You find me attractive, don't
          you, Dick? Please say you do.

He touches a hand to her cheek.

                    NASH
          Any man would.

                    VERONICA
          You mean that?

                    NASH
          I mean it.

She sighs and softens into him. Nash holds her with firm gentleness.

Breaking the spell, Veronica pushes away and lifts champagne from the ice
bucket, draining out the last dribble from the bottle.

                    VERONICA
          All gone - - like hope, draining
          away.

She slides a fresh bottle, holding it aloft.

                    VERONICA
          You any good with these things?

Nash takes the bottle and begins the opening process. Veronica pouts.

                    VERONICA
          What, no 'Don't you think you've
          had enough, old gel', sort of crap?

                    NASH
          I gave up handing out bullshit
          advice like that a long time ago.

                    VERONICA
          You'd leave me lying in the
          gutter? You are one mean
          son-of-a-bitch, you know that.

                    NASH
          What I'd do is pick you up, get
          you back on your feet. I've
          been there, don't worry.

                    VERONICA
             (with regret)
          I get the feeling I should have
          met you a long ways back.

                    NASH
          Well here I am now.

                    VERONICA
          And there's no time like the present,
          right?

                    NASH
          So they say.

                    VERONICA
          So this being the present there's
          no time like, where do we start?

Nash works the cork free with a dull plop and tops her glass.

                    NASH
          Tell me about Deborah.

                    VERONICA
             (shutting an eye)
          You mean like what color panties
          she wears?
             (grimacing)
          There I go again, me and my dirty
          mouth. But I was right all along.
          It sure is one screwball thing
          the pair of you have going.

                    NASH
          My interest in Deborah is only - -

                    VERONICA
          Professional - - sure it is. So
          let's be professional. You want
          to know about her? She's a phony.

                    NASH
          A phony?

                    VERONICA
          That's what I said. Last night
          we were out on the town with her
          lawyer man.

                    NASH
          You were with Norman Pargeter?

                    VERONICA
          The very same. Two against one.
          Not fair, not cricket, old boy.
          They thought they had the edge,
          but they were out a mile. Meow,
          meow, catty as all hell I am.
          I've been checking her out, and
          brother have I learned things.

                    NASH
          Go on.

                    VERONICA
          Got the man's interest. Okay,
          that top lofty Boston accent she
          hits you with: It's a fake. She
          hails from right here in Frisco,
          and I don't mean Nob Hill. See,
          I figure she has a first hubby
          stashed away somewhere and ergo
          her marriage to Creighton never
          was a marriage at all.

                    NASH
          What makes you suppose that?

                    VERONICA
          Oh, Dick, come on. You telling
          me there hasn't been a few sticky
          hands messing with the goods - -
          and stop looking like a cat hanging
          around a fish stall. She's smart and
          no mistake. I told Creighton what she
          was after, but he wouldn't listen.

                    NASH
          You mean his money?

                    VERONICA
          Well I don't mean his stamp
          collection - - sure, his money.
          What else?

                    NASH
          But you stayed with her.

                    VERONICA
          I did, and I'm not altogether sure
          why. Either way it was a mistake.
          I got a big scare thrown into me.
          You ever hear tell of a cop by
          the name of Bowman? - - What's
          wrong? You know this character?

                    NASH
          You had better tell me what
          happened.

                    VERONICA
               (shakes head)
          Let's just say he wandered
          beyond the plimsoll line.

Nash debates but decides not to push. He then takes out the small silver-
framed picture of the two boys on a rocking horse and shows it to Veronica.

                    NASH
          Tell me about these boys?

Veronica takes the picture and stares.

PHOTO OF TWO BOYS ON A ROCKING HORSE IN VERONICA'S HAND

                    NASH
          That's your brother, isn't it?
          - - or they both are.

Veronica nods sadly, fixing on the picture in her hand.

                    VERONICA
          Creighton and Leicester Dow. As
          alike as two peas in a pod, so it
          was said. Leicester died before
          I was born.

                    NASH
          How did he die?

                    VERONICA
          The subject was never discussed.
          That was Daddy's law - - the only
          law, as you might call it. You
          can't have missed seeing that
          damned painting.

                    NASH
          What you might call large.

                    VERONICA
          It belongs in a museum for sick
          egos. He was a louse, Dick, a
          bully and a tyrant - -

Veronica's words drift away, as SEGUE in FLASHBACK TO:

INT. YOUNG-PERSON'S BEDROOM - NIGHT

Pop music is playing and a GIRL of about sixteen is bop-dancing with a
YOUTH of about nineteen.

The Girl is a younger version of Veronica and wears a mini-skirt and vest
T-shirt. The guy is in jeans and T-shirt, and two other young guys hover in
a happy mood, taking turns to cut in and dance with her.

Sitting on the floor we see a YOUNG MAN of about twenty-four. This is a
younger version of Creighton. He is dressed stuffily in tie and jacket and
is trying to appear cool, grinning awkwardly and clapping his hands rather
clumsily in rhythm.

OUTER DOOR

The Door crashes open and an OLDER MAN stands menacingly in the doorframe.
This is ZACHARY DOW, as seen in the huge painting, now dressed in tweeds.

We fix on YOUNG CREIGHTON. All joy is wiped from his face. Fear takes its
place as he scrambles guiltily to his feet.

Veronica and the Youths stop dancing. With a face of puce fury, the Old Man
storms up to a cowering Creighton and begins to lay into him with powerful
open-handed blows. He then turns with fury to the Youths:

                    OLD MAN
          Get out! - - Get out, do
          you hear!

The Youths beat a fast exit. The Old Man turns and moves toward Veronica
with slow menace, forcing her back.

                    OLD MAN
          Lift up your skirt.

Veronica stares back in fear.

                    MAN
               (with brutal
               emphasis)
          Lift up your skirt, I said!

Veronica begins to meekly raise her skirt.

CUT TO YOUNG CREIGHTON

He watches, shocked, then giggles hysterically.

CUT TO OLD MAN'S GLARING, LASCIVIOUS EYES, as SEGUE BACK TO:

VERONICA RETURNING FROM HER REVERIE

She hands the picture back to Nash.

                    VERONICA
          I can't tell you anymore about
          Leicester. There was always a
          gloom around and could be his
          death held the key - - got a
          cigarette?

                    NASH
          Sorry, I'm trying to kick the
          habit.

                    VERONICA
          Wise man. Over there, if you
          wouldn't mind.

Nash collects cigarettes and a book of matches from off a coffee table and
lights her up.

                    NASH
          Was your brother homosexual?

                    VERONICA
          That's one from leftfield.

She draws on her cigarette thinking about it.

                    VERONICA
          My brother was one pretty mixed
          up character. If you want the
          full resume' try his shrink
          - - Doctor Naomi Fischer.

Nash brings out a notebook to jot this down.

                    VERONICA
          That's Fischer spelt the German
          way. She's a big wheel in the
          shrink business, and very choosy
          as to her clientele. Turned me
          down flat one time I needed help.
                  (beat)
          But to answer your question - -
          Creighton did put in a shift on the
          gay scene. Mainly though he got his
          kicks by proxy - - clickety-click,
          if you know what I mean.

Nash frowns, puzzled.

                    VERONICA
          Come on, Dick - - clickety-click.
          Creighton liked to take camera
          shots of a certain salty kind.
          Ask Deborah to show you the family
          album some time.

                    NASH
          You know this for sure?

                    VERONICA
          Oh, I know all my brother's
          little quirks. He grabbed most
          of the pot when the old bastard
          cashed in his chips then went out
          and wasted a bundle to finance
          my, ha ha, movie career.

She grabs for champagne and swills it back. Nash frowns watching her.

                    NASH
          I hear tell some of your stuff
          is pretty good.

                    VERONICA
          You want me to wet my knickers?
          You are a sweet man, Dick, and I
          thank you. But I have no illusions
          about the crap I fronted. Time was
          I ambition - - yeah. But Creighton
          soon nobbled that. All I had was
          slink, that's what he said.
               (crooks her finger)
          Know what? He's still saying it.

                    NASH
          Still?

Veronica laughs and closes with Nash and paws at him.

                    VERONICA
          Jesus, I'm near enough boxed.
               (nestles to him)
          Screwy thing is I want to try again.

                    NASH
          So why not? You look good enough
          to me.

                    VERONICA
          You must have come down from
          the stars. Too old, Dick.

                    NASH
          That's crazy, you're not old.

                    VERONICA
          But I am. In our world young
          means very young. When you hit
          thirty you are all washed up.
          Hold me, will you?

Nash draws her to him, and his CELL PHONE RINGS.

Veronica snatches away from Nash with stricken eyes.

                    NASH
          Only my phone.

He shows her the phone then holds it to his ear.

INT. GRACE CATHEDRAL - WHITMORE PHONING IN THE FOREGROUND

At back of Whitmore see police, forensic and media people milling.

                    WHITMORE
          Dick - - looks like we might
          have found Carmen. Got a body,
          the face all busted up.
INT. HOTEL ROOM

                              NASH
                    Where?

INT. GRACE CATHEDRAL

                         WHITMORE
                    You're gonna love this - -
                    Grace Cathedral. Jesus, she's
                    stark naked. Stretched out like
                    she's taking a sun bath.

INT. HOTEL ROOM

                         NASH
                    I'm on my way.

He closes off the call and pauses to digest Whitmore's news. Then he
remembers Veronica. She has drifted across the room and buried her face
into the folds of the curtain. He goes and draws her to him.

                         NASH
                    You been getting some bad
                    calls?

She comes around into his arms.

                         VERONICA
                    I thought - -

                         NASH
                    What did you think, Veronica?

                         VERONICA
                    If I told you, you would know
                    for sure I'd gone mad. Maybe I
                    have.
                         (muffled into
                         his shirt)
                    You are going.

                         NASH
                    I have to.

She clings desperately to him. Nash trails fingers along her hairline and
kisses her forehead. She tilts her head for him to kiss her mouth. Nash
delivers a brief, tender kiss. She sighs, reaches and kisses him again, the
kiss becoming passionate.

Next they are in the throes of preliminary love-making, as DISSOLVE TO:

EXT. ESTABLISHING SHOT OF GRACE CATHEDRAL - EVENING

See much activity, crowds milling, blue police lights flashing etc.

INT. REAR HALLWAY OF CATHEDRAL

Connor stands addressing the media, a mobile TV camera in evidence. To the
side priests and wardens stare with shocked disbelief. He sees Nash
battling through, says a last few words and moves to meet him. They are
joined by Whitmore. Both Connor and Whitmore send Nash doubting looks.

                              NASH
                    Sorry Chief, I got held up.
                    What's the score?

Connor studies Nash for a moment.

                              CONNOR
                    Let's get some air.

Whitmore leaves them to it as they move away.

EXT. PARKWAY ADJACENT TO GRACE CATHEDRAL - CONTINUOUS

Connor and Nash halt at the lip of the Park.

                              CONNOR
                    Could be we've found the missing
                    servant - - right age, ethnic
                    type. Problem is the corpse is
                    practically unrecognizable.

                              NASH
                    It's her, gotta be. Fits with Dow.

                              CONNOR
                    Not quite. She was strangled not
                    clubbed to death - - with something
                    thin and strong, like piano wire.
                    And there isn't the same rage in
                    evidence. This is a cold-blooded
                    act, the features obliterated
                    with systematic precision.

                              NASH
                    To wipe out her identity.

                              CONNOR
                    I'd say so.

                              NASH
                    I still say it's her.

                              CONNOR
                    We'll know in due course - -
                    but God! He near enough wiped
                    the slate clean. Even ripped
                    off her earrings.

                              NASH
                    Some joker.

                              CONNOR
                    He's got balls, I'll give him
                    that. Took her in one of the
                    colonnades. Dragged her into a
                    robing chamber, where the priests
                    and choirboys get rigged out.
                    Found by a young curate, who
                    isn't doing too well right now.

                                                          56

                    NASH
          He's buying time, Brian.

                    CONNOR
          But time for what?
               (beat)
          Anything you need to tell me?

                    NASH
          The sister - - something not
          right there.

                    CONNOR
          The actress, you mean?

                    NASH
          She's one troubled lady, and
          not solely on account of her
          brother. I can't pin it but
          there's a worm gnawing at her.

                    CONNOR
          Seems the least of our worries
          right now. Watch your step, Dick.
          Don't get emotionally involved.
          These movie queens live in their
          own make-believe world.

                    NASH
          Yeah - -

He ponders on it, as DISSOLVE TO:

INT. OAK-PANELED ROOM - DAY

Deborah stands back to a tall bay wind bay window. She is dressed in a
tasteful black two-piece suit and holds a glass of brown sherry at chest
height. The expression on her face is cold and it is evident she fighting
hard to contain her anger.

We follow Deborah's gaze above a long polished table strewn with portfolios
and legal papers to the far end of the Room. Where Veronica, dressed
brazenly, stands near flirting with two lawyers.

To the side, Norman Pargeter stands head bowed. Forced to meet Deborah's
hard stare, he trudges reluctantly up to her and mutters:

                    PARGETER
          We can still contest.

                    DEBORAH
          Can we.

                    PARGETER
          Of course, of course. I do fear,
          however, that we may have been
          over- ambitious - - yes, I see
          that now.

                    DEBORAH
          You misled me.

                    PARGETER
          I - I only followed your instructions.

Deborah seers him with cold contempt, then turns to front again.

                    DEBORAH
          The impressionist paintings
          stung most.

                    PARGETER
          Deborah, please believe I share
          your disappointment. But you have
          scarcely come out a pauper. You
          retain possession of the house
          and have a very worthy portfolio
          of stocks and shares to your name.
          By any measure you are now a young
          woman of considerable wealth.

                    DEBORAH
          So I am not to complain.

                    PARGETER
          I am only urging caution. In due
          course we will make an assessment
          of the situation.

A nerve jumps and he jabs a finger at his cheekbone to arrest it, which
Deborah notices.

                    DEBORAH
          What is wrong with you?

                    PARGETER
          Why, nothing. I am perfectly fine.

                    DEBORAH
          You look anything but perfectly
          fine. You look like a dead fish.

                    PARGETER
          Clearly I am perturbed by the
          outcome.

She frowns, measuring him.

                    DEBORAH
          No it is more than that.

She then switches to Veronica, taking a sustaining breath.

                    DEBORAH
          I suppose I had better congratulate
          the winner.

Pargeter delays her with a cautionary hand.

                    PARGETER
          Choose your words with care,
          Deborah.

She brushes him aside and walks head erect toward Veronica, the glass of sherry held with a steady hand. Veronica registers her approach and they meet face to face at center of the room.

                         DEBORAH
               Congratulations.

                         VERONICA
               Thanks, and to you. Fair result
               all round, I thought.

                         DEBORAH
               Was it?

                         VERONICA
               Well, nobody comes out broke.

                         DEBORAH
                  (bites her lip)
               The paintings are very dear to
               me. I had quite some involvement
               in their purchase.

                         VERONICA
               So what are you saying? You got
               the house. Want to barter?

                         DEBORAH
               The house was Creighton's. It
               is only right that it should
               come to me.

                         VERONICA
               To be accurate - - Baronmore, as
               pop was fond of calling it - - was
               my family home from when I was a
               kid. I never held to Creighton
               getting sole rights.

                         DEBORAH
               I won't part with the house.

                         VERONICA
               Then be satisfied. From where I
               stand you come out in pretty good
               shape for a gal working her ass
               off in an accounts office less
               than two years ago.

Deborah stiffens.

                         DEBORAH
               You have been investigating me.

                         VERONICA
               You guessed it, and you know what?
               Five minutes ago I was ready to call
               it quits. Now seeing you for the
               selfish little plunderer you are,
               I've changed my mind.

Deborah struggles to contain her anger.

>   DEBORAH
>   You are disgusting.

>   VERONICA
>   Call it any way you want. But your
>   act never fooled me. I'm on to you
>   Deborah - or Jean or whatever your
>   name is. All I need is that one
>   last little piece of the jigsaw.
>   Know the one I mean? The one that
>   tells you have a first husband
>   somewhere. Then the party will
>   be well and truly over.

Deborah tosses the sherry she is holding in Veronica's face.

The room jerks silent. Startled eyes fix on the two women, who stand face to face in bitter confrontation.

Then Veronica grins.

>   VERONICA
>   Feel better now?

The lawyers converge on them. Veronica takes a proffered handkerchief. Sherry is splashed over her dress and face. A deathly pale Pargeter leads Deborah quickly away. As he does, Deborah twists around to see Veronica leaving, escorted by the lawyers blubbing their apologies.

EXT. TAXI WAITING IN DRIVE

Deborah smiles her thanks to the lawyers, who have followed her outside, and climbs into the Taxi. One of them closes the door.

INT. TAXI

>   VERONICA
>   Go.

The driver pulls away as directed. With the Taxi on the move, Veronica crumples into the seat, her smile vanishing.

Distantly hear the driver: "Where to, lady?"

A tear escapes and runs down Veronica's cheek, as DISSOLVE TO:

EXT. IRON GATES OF DOW ESTATE - DAY

Nash tests the Gates, which are locked. Behind see his parked car. He then presses the call button set in a column. No answer comes back from the squawk box. He steps back and looks around. Then hear distant CAR MOTOR.

On the drive beyond a car approaches at speed. It draws to a halt and Grant Bowman steps out. Seeing Nash, he grins and walks up to the gate.

>   GRANT
>   Well look who's here. G'day
>   to you, sport. Now what the
>   fuck do you want?

                    NASH
          I could ask you the same thing.

                    GRANT
          Oh, full of our little self
          today, are we? I seem to recall
          advising you to keep your nose
          out of things what don't concern
          you.

                    NASH
          Trouble is I find they do concern
          me. You got the way in?

                    GRANT
          Sure.
                (takes out
                zapper)
          Clever little doings. You point
          it at the magic eye up there and
          the gates swing open all by
          themselves.

                    NASH
          Good, open up. I got business inside.

                    GRANT
          And what might the nature of this
          business be exactly?

                    NASH
          Police business.

                    GRANT
          Well now, seeing as how I represent
          the police interest in these parts
          - - how can I put this? Piss off.

                    NASH
          I don't propose arguing with you,
          Bowman. Mrs Dow is expecting me.

                    GRANT
          No she ain't - - cause she ain't
          at home. So that being the case
          I'd say your presence is redundant.

                    NASH
          This could land you in trouble,
          Bowman. You want that, after
          what went down before?

Grant stops and paws at his mouth.

                    GRANT
          Been reaming the muck, have we?

                    NASH
          You could put it that way. Got
          yourself quite a reputation, of
          sorts.

                    GRANT
         What, jostlin' a few spades?
         What's that amount to?

                    NASH
         Not much by your terms I shouldn't
         think. Only I heard different. Way
         I heard tell you were something of
         a ladies' man, in your own twisted
         kind of way. Lucky for you the officer
         in question was married and didn't
         want to press charges.

                    GRANT
         Nice sense of humor you got
         there, sport.

                    NASH
         Yeah, now open up.

Grant is tempted, but good sense prevails and he grins at Nash.

                    GRANT
         There'd be no point. Like I say,
         the lady's not around. Gone off
         to the races for the day by the
         look of it. And I got better things
         to attend to.
              (makes to turn)

                    NASH
         You hear about the body found last
         night? Woman all mashed up.

                    GRANT
              (stopping)
         What's that to me?

                    NASH
         I got a notion it's Carmen, the
         servant we've been looking for.

                    GRANT
         I don't see out how I'm meant
         to figure in this. But you're
         out a mile. She's back.

                    NASH
         Back? What do you mean?

                    GRANT
         You have trouble with English
         when you was in school? The dago,
         she's back there in the house.
         I saw her not ten minutes ago.

                    NASH
         This some kind of put-on?

                    GRANT
          Now what makes you think I'm so
          all-fired eager to put you on?
          Look, mate, you can believe what
          you want, but what I'm tellin'
          you is so. Her stuff's there in
          her room. I was about to pay my
          respects when you butted in.

                    NASH
          If this is on the level I need
          to see her.

                    GRANT
              (grinning)
          Why, want to ask if she's the
          one found dead in that big
          church?

                    NASH
          Open this gate.

                    GRANT
          Huh-huh. You got no jurisdiction
          around here, Nash. So if you don't
          mind I'll be sayin' ta-ta.

Nash weighs it, then nods and takes a step back.

                    NASH
          All right. But we are going
          to talk again.

                    GRANT
          You could just be right there,
          sport.

They stand eyeballing one another, as DISSOLVE TO:

INT. DARKENED MOVIE THEATRE

This is of the compact kind that show fringe, non-mainstream movies. On the
screen see - COLORS - NOISE - GIANT FACE OF YOUNG WOMAN.

CUT TO VERONICA

She is seated near the back of the theatre, absorbed with the movie.
She turns not wanting to, and along the empty row see:

DARKENED SEATED FIGURE

SCREEN

Music swells with dramatic effect, as a Young Woman - call her THE GIRL -
walks with great trepidation up marbled steps toward:

HUGE DOOR

The Girl is very young and exudes innocence. She is dressed in Edwardian
riding gear, with a black bowler angled on her head and carries a riding
crop. Her blonde air is fashioned in a chignon.

                                                              63

                         CAMP VOICE
                        FROM AUDIENCE
                Watch out behind you, love - -
                that's how I first got it.

The sparse audience responds with spontaneous LAUGHTER and CATCALLS.

CUT TO VERONICA - she begins to drift.

SCREEN

The Girl comes up to the Door and reaches in fear for iron ring handle
hanging from the mouth of a GRINNING GARGOYLE, her gloved hand stalling.

Her feared gaze lifts to see GOTHIC SPIRES of the SINISTER CASTLE she is
about to enter. Overhead, dark clouds swirl across a black sky.

The Girl again reaches takes hold of the ring. She twists and the catch
clanks with releases. She hesitates and then pushes the Door creaks, which
open a few inches and a WISP OF STEAM exits.

Hesitant, very frightened, the Girl pushes, needing to bring her shoulder
to the task, until there is just enough space to squeeze through to:

VAST HALL

The Girl stares up and around with feared eyes. The ceiling disappears into
high blackness. FLAMED TORCHES burn on stone walls.

She goes slowly forward toward:

DARK ARCHWAY

Reaching the Arch, she halts.

CUT TO PILLAR

A SMALL UGLY HAND slither around, this followed a moment later by a second
hand. More hands appear, until the pillar is infested with these gnarled
hands, which writhe like spiders.

Next GRINNING DWARF FACES peep out from around the pillar.

The Girl snatches around but sees nothing as the Dwarfs duck back.

She reaches for a silver crucifix hanging around her neck and again goes
toward the Arch.

PILLAR

The Dwarfs, about five, scurry out, tiptoeing behind her.

DARK ARCHWAY

The Girl halts, unable to take another step. The Dwarfs pan out behind her.
One of them snickers. She sees them as her gaze lowers and screams.

CUT TO VERONICA

She clamps a hand to her mouth, snatching at the seat in front.

SCREEN

The Dwarfs snare the Girl. She beats at them with her riding crop. Torn from her hand. She beats at them with her gloved-hands and kicks and screams as they overpower her. The Dwarfs pull away her tunic, shirt, petticoats, boots, making guttural sounds of glee.

Stripped, they lift and carry her shoulder high through the Arch, when all at once the Dwarfs' jollity disappears, as they enter:

SATANIC CHAPEL

The Girl is now mute with terror.

Black curtains are draped on the walls, where more torches burn. Above a STONE ALTAR a gigantic a curtain is blazoned in the SIGN OF THE GOAT.

The Dwarfs march the terrified Girl to the Altar. Red velvet cords are in readiness and they fasten her down, arms and legs spread like a starfish.

The Dwarfs again become excited, mocking and prodding the girl with gnarled fingers. One wearing the Girl's bowler becomes manic, grunting and reaching to unbuckle his belt. The other Dwarfs slap him back. They squabbled around then fall silent, all their bravado gone.

With fingers to lips, they silently melt from view as TENSION MUSIC builds.

CUT TO VERONICA

There is a rustled movement and then an OBSCURE FIGURE seats beside her. She flinches but holds her gaze on the screen.

An arm clamps her shoulder, then see:

HAND WITH WHITE PAD

SCREEN: BLACK CURTAINS IN FOCUS

The Curtains part, and through the Darkness see:

LARGE INHUMAN EYE

The Eye expands, bulged with bloodied capillaries.

CUT TO GIRL'S TERRIFIED FACE

THE EYE

A crack forms on the PUPIL and begins to spread.

The Eye splits. Blood oozes. FLOODING. RED.

CUT TO HAND WITH WHITE PAD

The Pad comes around, expanding finally to BLACKNESS.

EXT. DISTANCE SHOT OF GATES TO DOW ESTATE - BECOMING DARK

Nash watches from his parked car as the Gates swing open. A car drives out and stops. Grant gets out and closes the gates with his zapper. He peers up and around. He then gets back into his car and drives away.

Nash watches Grant's car disappear. He then gets out, and spying a breach, he moves in that direction.

EXT. GROUNDS OF THE ESTATE

Nash emerges through the gap. He stands some forty yards from the rear of the House. He switches his gaze to the distant Pavilion then starts toward the House.

EXT. PERMITER PATH OF HOUSE.

Nash works his way around, pausing to peer in windows. He comes to a sudden stop, snapping his upward gaze to:

HIGH WINDOW

From Nash's p.o.v. flimsy white curtains drift at an open window, obscuring what may be a FIGURE moving back.

                                                    DISSOLVE TO:

EXT. TRAILER IN SLOPING HOLLOW - DARKNESS SETTING IN

Deborah climbs from her sportcar and focuses on the Trailer. This is a large but dilapidated structure. A dim lamp burns above the door but no lights show from inside.

Deborah glances anxiously around. She then approaches the door, hesitates, then raps with a knuckle and calls:

                        DEBORAH
              Grant?

No reply comes back. She glances behind quickly then fishes in her purse and brings out a key and lets herself in.

INTERIOR OF TRAILER

Deborah flicks the light switch and glances around to see a galley kitchen, a couple of closed doors, the main room living area of the trailer.

The galley kitchen in cluttered disgustingly and Deborah makes a distasteful mouth. She again delves in her purse and brings out a small silver automatic handgun. She releases the safety catch and returns the gun to her purse and then casts around in earnest, searching.

Her gaze lights on a door. She takes a breath, crosses and goes into:

BEDROOM OF TRAILER

She stops, taking in an unmade cot bed, a chipboard wardrobe, and much untidiness. She opens the wardrobe to see jackets and various clothing items crammed hanging on the rail plus a mound of stuff on the base. She backs off with distaste and leaves the Bedroom.

LIVING AREA

She takes in a superlarge TV and music center, a sparse easy chair mounded with clothes, a thin curtain drooping above the one small window. Strewn over a basic couch and floor there are a number of GIRLIE MAGAZINES.

Deborah picks up one of the Mags, rifles pages, tosses it aside. She picks up and does likewise with a second then. Frustrated, her head twists, and pinned on a nail we see:

SINGLE PAGE GIRLIE PICTURE

Deborah tensely goes across to take a better look.

The girl in the picture is very young. She has extravagantly blonde waving hair and wears a sou'wester and black thigh length waders and nothing else. A fishing rod is propped over her right shoulder and a fish dangles on a line behind her.

A harsh sound rattles in Deborah's throat. She reaches clawed hands to tear the picture from the nail and then savagely tears it into pieces and dashes them to the floor.

She glares down with hate, as DISSOLVE TO:

INT. ENTRANCE TO DOW MANSION HOUSE - NIGHT CLOSING IN

Nash enters, looking around. The House is silent. His gaze flashes over the giant painting of Zachary Dow. Nash moves to the staircase and begins to climb, reaching:

LANDING

He pauses, and we see from his p.o.v. -

CORRIDOR WITH BEDROOM DOORS - ONE DOOR PART-OPEN

Nash walks to the Door, cautiously pushed it wide and enters:

BEDROOM

Plain room, as described. Set on the bed is an open valise.

Nash registers the open window, white curtains drifting. He crosses to peer down to see where he had been standing. He leaves the window and goes into:

BATHROOM

This is a small basic affair. A wicker laundry basket stands in a corner.

Nash pulls back the shower curtain. The floor is wet and the shower-head drips. He goes to the wicker basket and lifts the lid to see items of female underwear dumped. Nash returns to the Bedroom and exits to:

CORRIDOR - AT FAR END A TALL WHITE DOOR

Nash ponders then goes toward the door and enters:

MASTER BEDROOM

As described, the room is large and airy. A grand ladies' dressing table stands close to the bed. A glass-doored wardrobe fills one wall.

Nash slides back a glass door to find an array of expensive gowns etc. He opens a drawer and lifts out a scanty item of lingerie. Guiltily, he slams shut the drawer and the glass door and quickly leaves.

SERIES OF MERGING SHOTS:

Nash heads down the staircase followed by gaze of Old Zachary Dow.

EXT. HOUSE AS NASH LEAVES - NIGHT SETTING IN

Nash pauses to peer toward distant Pavilion. He moves in that direction.

EXT.PAVILION

Nash enters to:

INT. PAVILION

Nash switches lights and gazes around, settling on the ancient phonograph. The lid is raised and he gazes down at the turntable to see:

OLD COLUMBIA 78 - JOHNNY RAY - PLEASE MR SUN

Nash pensively exits, turning off the lights.

EXT. PAVILION - NIGHT NOW FIRMLY SET IN

Nash's gaze freezes as he stares at:

YELLOW LIGHT SHOWING UPSTAIRS FROM HOUSE - -

                                        DISSOLVE TO:

INT. TRAILER - NIGHT

Deborah faces the door, her fear evident. Hear gravel crunch. The door opens and Grant bursts in. Seeing Deborah he grins and lets his eyes run over her in a sleazy way. Deborah tries to cover her nervousness:

                    DEBORAH
          I have been waiting for you,
          Grant.

                    GRANT
          So I see.

He goes up to her and strokes the back of a hand lazily over cheek.

                    GRANT
          So how we come out?

Deborah twists her head away from his touch.

                    DEBORAH
          Keep your distance.

                    GRANT
          Why, nobody's watchin'.

                    DEBORAH
          We can't take chances.

                    GRANT
          Is that right?

Grinning, he walks to the couch and lifts a cushion and peers underneath.

                    GRANT
          Nope, looks like we're all by
          our little selves - - less you
          want to count the roaches.

He then notices the torn picture and stoops to retrieve the pieces,
pretending to match them together.

                    GRANT
          Ain't right, destroying other
          folk's property. This was my
          all-time favourite. (grins)
          I always did wonder what you
          had in mind to do with that
          stinky old fish.

He balls up the pieces and shoots them away. As he ambles back toward her,
Deborah's hands clutch at her purse. Grant pauses, noticing this.

                    GRANT
          Get rid of Rita Hayworth?

                    DEBORAH
          Yes, she's gone. Not without
          leaving her mark.

                    GRANT
          Her mark, what's that mean?

                    DEBORAH
          He left her my paintings,
          damn him!

                    GRANT
          What, that hippy weirdo shit?

                    DEBORAH
          No, the collection of Impressionist
          works I spent ages collecting.
          Gone to that - - obscenity!

                    GRANT
          Worth much?

                    DEBORAH
          Priceless - - but that isn't
          the point!

Grant turns that over.

                    GRANT
          You get the house?

                    DEBORAH
          The house - - stocks, bonds.
          Wealth by your terms.

                    GRANT
          But not by yours, that it?

                    DEBORAH
          By mine, too - - yes.

                    GRANT
          Then forget it. You got money
          and you got the house. Seems
          to me you could turn around
          and buy a whole new batch of
          art shit if you wanted.

                    DEBORAH
          I could.

                    GRANT
          Let's face it, you're just a
          spoilt little lady.

Deborah makes no reply and Grant eyes become shrewd.

                    GRANT
          Only there's more, ain't there?

                    DEBORAH
          She's had me investigated!

                    GRANT
          Investigated?

                    DEBORAH
          She knows all about me - - my
          background. I'm going to lose
          everything!

                    GRANT
          Keep your hair on. You were his
          wife, common law or otherwise.
          She's bluffin'.
               (savouring)
          Gravy ride starts here. Which
          being the case you and me need
          to get things settled, Jeanie.

                    DEBORAH
          Don't call me that! Not ever!

                    GRANT
          There you go again, getting
          yourself all riled up over
          stuff that don't matter. Ain't
          nothing to a name. I'll call
          you the Duchess of Donk if it
          suits. So long as I get my dues.

                    DEBORAH
          Look - - this has got to be - -

                    GRANT
          Last throw of the dice, that
          what you mean? Cripes, it's
          like you never want to see my
          hide again. You sure know how   (CONT'D)

                    to be hurtful. But got to tell
                    you, girl. The show's set to
                    run and run.

Deborah glares at him, speechless with hate.

                          GRANT
                    I'd advise getting that mean
                    look out of them big blue eyes.
                    Brings on wrinkles, squinting
                    like that. It's time my backside
                    was somewhere else, no need to
                    concern yourself on that count.
                    But you'll be hearing from me,
                    good and regular.

Saying this, he takes off his jacket and starts to unbutton his shirt.

                          DEBORAH
                    What are you doing?

                          GRANT
                    Just making myself comfy - -
                    Oh, the maid's back.

                          DEBORAH
                    Carmen? But that can't be.

                          GRANT
                    Why can't it? Jesus H Christ.
                    What's the big deal about some
                    half-arsed domestic? She's there,
                    take my word for it. Plus that
                    snoopy Nash bastard. Said you'd
                    agreed to talk to him, that right?
                    Found another body, thought it was
                    the dago.
                         (beat)
                    What's-a-mater now?

Deborah stands eyes glazed. Grant scans her face with a hand then shakes
his head. He starts to peel off his shirt, which jars Deborah back to the
moment.

                          GRANT
                    Might take a gander at the old
                    town - - yeah. Wonder if the
                    Stoned Crow's still goin'
                    strong?

                          DEBORAH
                    You agreed to one final payment.

                          GRANT
                    What I said ain't worth chickenshit.
                    Now you listen here, Miss Fancy
                    Drawers. I took some' big fuckin
                    risks for you. Remember, Joey-boy,
                    your first wed?

                    DEBORAH
          I never wanted that.

                     GRANT
          Ain't you the little hypocrite?
          You wanted it all right. How else
          you figure to get rid of the little
          prick? Think I just sidled up and
          tucked a fifty note in his top
          pocket? Get real.

                    DEBORAH
          How do I know you are telling
          the truth?

Grant wipes sweat from his big chest and tosses the shirt aside.

                     GRANT
          Heard from Joe lately? Be a
          big surprise if you had. It's
          done, and more.

                    DEBORAH
          What do you mean?

                     GRANT
          Now what you think I mean? If
          you want to know, I got fed-up
          of that ponce swankin' around
          in his silk pyjamas, callin'
          the shots.

Deborah weighs this. Her eyes narrow.

                    DEBORAH
          This time I know you are lying.
          You were with me, remember?

                     GRANT
          Not at the critical point I
          weren't. Which kind of puts
          your star-gazing tale into
          what you might call the dubious
          category. Don't look so worried.
          The grunt works over. All you
          got to do is keep me sweet and
          it's roses all the way.
               (grins, lecherous)
          Speaking of which, I wouldn't
          mind smellin' a rose right now.

Saying this he moves toward her with clear intent.

                     GRANT
          Mourning black, suits you.
          Goes clear down to basics,
          I'm betting.

                    DEBORAH
             (backing away)
          No!

Her eyes darted left to right as Grant nears. Next the small automatic is in her hand, pointing at him. Grant stops and looks at the gun.

                    GRANT
          Well, now.

                    DEBORAH
          All my life I have been used
          by men. No more. Believe me,
          I will shoot if I have to.

                    GRANT
          I think I do believe you. Be a
          right tom-tit not to, wouldn't I?

                    DEBORAH
          One last payment - - as agreed.

                    GRANT
          Okay - - got it with you?

                    DEBORAH
          I - I have it ready - - at the
          house.

                    GRANT
          Good enough.
            (moves forward)
          Except you know it ain't gonna
          be the finale. Well, not less
          you can pull that trigger.

Deborah flinches as he pushes his belly to the nozzle of the gun.

                    GRANT
          It's make your mind up time.

Deborah glares with hate but is unable to shoot. Grant grins and takes a grip on her wrist and twists. Deborah gives a faint cry as he prises the gun free. He tosses it aside and yanks her to him.

                    DEBORAH
          No - -

Grant smears her face with his mouth then wrenches the jacket back from her shoulder. In the same movement, he scoops and carries her to dump her on the couch.

Deborah makes a whimpering sound as Grant comes down over her -

                                        DISSOLVE TO:

INT. NAOMI FISCHER'S STUDY - NIGHT

The room is crowded in Bohemian fashion, with books and files crammed untidily in bookcases and stacked in piles on the floor.

Naomi enters, clicks on a desk lamp and goes around the desk to sit. She is a large-boned handsome woman in her early forties. She wears a baggy jumper and black stretch pants and displays rows of beads around her neck. Nash follows on into the room and stands facing her.

                    NAOMI
          I will tell you straight off,
          Inspector, that I doubt if I
          will be able to help you.
               (holds aloft
               cigarettes)
          Any objections?

                    NASH
               (glancing around)
          They're your lungs.

Naomi smiles and lights up.

                    NAOMI
          So how did you find me? - -
          sit, pull up that chair.

Nash drags up the chair indicated and sits facing her.

                    NASH
          I found you through Veronica
          Dow.

                    NAOMI
          And what did she tell you?

                    NASH
          Among other things, that you
          turned her down when she sought
          your help.

Naomi draws and blows smoke, measuring her response.

                    NAOMI
          To be accurate, I counseled
          her for a period. It became
          apparent, however, that she
          was playing games. It was
          clearly a waste of my time.

                    NASH
          Well, I guess you know your
          trade.

                    NAOMI
          I have little patience with
          faux hysterics, Nash. My hours
          are too valuable.

                    NASH
          But the rule didn't apply to
          her brother.

                    NAOMI
          Are you admonishing me?
               (nods)
          You are nevertheless right.
          Creighton did measure as an
          interesting subject. I am not
          certain I can go any further.   (CONT'D)

                    Even with death the trust
                    between doctor and patient
                    is sacrosanct.

                              NASH
                    What about the trust with
                    future murder victims? There
                    have already been two pretty
                    grim homicides connected with
                    Creighton Dow. Isn't that enough
                    to warrant a breach of ethics?

                              NAOMI
                    The second being the Murder
                    in the Cathedral, I take it.
                    Are you certain of this? I
                    wasn't aware a connexion
                    had been established.

                              NASH
                    Let's say I'm working on that
                    assumption.

Naomi ponders then reaches into a drawer and brings out a bottle of scotch
and two large whisky glasses. She sloshes out a couple of good measures and
slides one across to Nash.

                              NAOMI
                    All right, let us see - -
                    take a drink. That is pure
                    malt. You look as if you
                    need it.

Naomi drinks and Nash follows suit, coughing slightly. She sits back
smoking and studies him.

                              NAOMI
                    You have first a question. I
                    see it hanging on the tip of
                    your tongue. You want to ask
                    if Creighton Dow might not be
                    dead. Am I correct?

Nash stares across at her.

                              NASH
                    Is it possible?

                              NAOMI
                    Most anything is. Whether it
                    is likely is an altogether
                    different matter.
                        (takes a draw)
                    But taking it for the moment
                    you are right, it would appear
                    to raises two further questions.
                    First, why Creighton would want
                    to falsify his own demise. And
                    the second larger conundrum of
                    who has taken his place in death.

                              NASH
             That's right.
                  (grimaces)
             I was as sure as dammit the
             body in the church belonged
             to a Mexican servant we've
             been searching for. Now it
             seems she's back.

                              NAOMI
             Seems?

                              NASH
             The evidence says as much. Her
             things are there in her room,
             I checked it out myself. But
             no Mexican servant.

Naomi crushes out her cigarette in a copper ashtray and immediately lights
a second.

                              NAOMI
             The easiest proposition, Nash,
             is the one that convinces us
             we are right.

                              NASH
             Am I fooling myself? All right,
             but I've come this far. I have
             to see it through.
                  (beat)
             Can't you help me out here, Doc?

Naomi ponders then wedges on a pair of steel-framed glasses and reaches for
a manila folder. She opens the folder and peruses notes.

                              NAOMI
             Veronica was Creighton's most
             significant other - - do you
             understand the term?

                              NASH
             The one he related to above
             all others, you mean?

                              NAOMI
             Yes, well put.

                              NASH
             More so than his wife?

                              NAOMI
             Oh, yes, considerably more.
             Creighton's marriage was only
             ever a façade, a sham in truth.

                              NASH
             What about him once having been
             a twin? How does that figure?

Naomi removes her glasses and gazes at Nash with wry amusement.

                    NAOMI
          You gleaned this from Veronica,
          of course.

Nash shifts uncomfortably in his chair. Naomi smiles as if reading his
thoughts and refits her glasses and returns to the file.

                    NAOMI
          Though you are not correct in
          saying Creighton was once a
          twin. Twins are twins throughout
          their lives, even as in this case
          when death intervenes. They were
          monozygotic, Creighton and his
          brother, which is to say they
          were as genetically identical
          as two human beings can possibly
          be. The loss therefore was akin
          to the surviving twin being
          sundered from half of himself.

                    NASH
          So where does Veronica fit in?

                    NAOMI
          Veronica took the place of the
          lost brother and between them
          they put up a united front
          against their father, whom
          they both feared and hated.

                    NASH
          Veronica said he was a louse.

                    NAOMI
          Yes, a deeply troubled man,
          to be sure.

                    NASH
          Was Creighton capable of murder? - -
          in your opinion.

                    NAOMI
          Most everyone is, wouldn't you
          say? If you are asking if he
          showed signs of homicidal
          tendencies - -
               (ponders)
          With hindsight it is seductive
          to think so. Though I am not
          certain - -

She draws and puffs smoke, coming to a decision.

                    NAOMI
          You should know that I counseled
          Creighton the afternoon of his
          murder. Assuming your theory to
          be wrong.

                    NASH
          Why didn't you come forward
          with this?

                    NAOMI
          I saw no good reason to. I
          value my privacy, Nash. The
          session adhered to the usual
          pattern. Neurotic doubt followed
          by supreme egotism. There was
          no indication of any impending
          calamity.

                    NASH
          I'm too tired to argue.

He knocks back his scotch and sets the empty glass down.

                    NASH
          I know you think I'm off my
          crust. But if Creighton is
          still alive, logic says you
          would be top of the list for
          a visit.

                    NAOMI
               (smokes calmly)
          In the event I believe I would
          be capable of dealing with him.

                    NASH
          I hope you are right - -

Fix on Nash's troubled face, as DISSOLVE TO:-

EXT. STEPS LEADING TO UP-MARKET TOWN HOUSE - FRONT DOOR AJAR - NIGHT

Move toward Door and continue on through a tastefully decorated hall and
down a short run of steps to a second open door and enter a cozy book-lined
study, where Norman Pargeter sits sprawled behind his desk. He is gaping
hideously, his THROAT SLASHED.

INT. DEBORAH DOW'S BEDROOM - NIGHT

Deborah, eyes closed, leans panting back to the door. Her shirt blouse is
torn at the shoulder.

She then moves from the door and limps to and her bathroom. Hear the tub
being filled. Deborah comes out wearing a terrycloth bathrobe. With water
still running, she sits at her dressing table.

Deborah peers into her mirror and tenderly fingers her lips and eases the
robe from off her left shoulder, where a bruised area shows. Folding the
robe in place, she takes up a hairbrush and begins to brush absently at her
hair, suddenly pausing.

Dismissing her fears, she takes up the hairbrush and makes a few absent
strokes, pausing again as a THIN TRAIL OF CIGARETTE SMOKE waft past her.

She reaches with a trembling hand to angle a mirror flange to see:

MAN SITTING WATCHING FROM CORNER OF THE ROOM

His image is obscured by gloom, but see he wears a tuxedo and has one leg crossed comfortably over the other. Smoke drifts upward from a cigarette held within a holder. His face is stiffly white, smirking an amused smirk.

Deborah comes twisting to her feet and stares with unbelieving eyes at the seated figure. He then speaks in the effeminate voice of Creighton Dow:

                    CREIGHTON
          Trading rough again, darling?

Deborah takes a step toward him, groping to keep her balance.

                    CREIGHTON
          Whatever is wrong, darling? You
          look as if you have seen a ghost.

With this, he laughs a braying laugh.

Deborah takes one faltering step forward. She chokes, unable to breath, reaching out a hand. Then pitches forward in a dead faint.

EXT. SALOON CAR - NIGHT

The Car is parked in a hidden place, a canyon or tree-bordered lane.

Focus on trunk, where from inside hear THUD.

EXT. GRANT'S TRAILER - NIGHT - NASH'S CAR DRAWING UP

Nash gets out and warily approaches the Trailer.
A dimmed light seeps through a chink in the curtain. Nash raps once on the door and calls:

                    NASH
          Bowman?

No reply comes back. Nash takes out his handgun and tries the door, and finding it unlocked goes inside to:

INTERIOR OF TRAILER

Nash gazes around taking in the galley kitchen etc. He puts away his gun and moves to the living area, taking stock of the TV etc. He notices the girlie mags, lifts one from the couch, flicks pages and tosses it back. He moves and enters:

BEDROOM

Nash goes to the wardrobe and searches around. Finding nothing, he turns to the dishevelled cot bed, getting down on one knee to peer underneath.

See as Nash sees a jumble of clothes and empty cigarette packets etc. There is also a large BOOK and SHOEBOX. Nash reaches these out then sits on the bed and examines the book, which we see titled:

THE WORLD'S MOST POWERFUL RIFLES AND HANDGUNS

Nash turns a few pages, set the Book aside, and opens the Shoebox. Layered on top see:

LARGE COLOR PHOTOGRAPHS

Nash examines these, to see:

FLASH SHOTS OF DEBORAH AND GRANT PHYSICALLY ENTANGLED

Nash smiles thinly. He then delves into the shoebox and brings out:

QUARTO-SIZED BUFF ENVELOPE

He unfastens the holding clip and withdraws a batch of documents, together with a press cutting and wallet. He unfolds a document to see:

CERTIFICATE OF MARRIAGE

Travel down the document, to see:

SEPTEMBER 10 2004. JOSEPH CARL AVERY, CAR MECHANIC, 26, Married JEAN JENNIFER MILLS, STUDENT, 16, at 3.30 pm at MISSION ROCK REGISTRY OFFICE.

Nash opens the wallet. Behind the cellophane window, see:

MUGSHOT of DARK-HAIRED BALDING MAN OF ABOUT THIRTY-FIVE

In the panel next to this is an ID stating:

JOSEPH CARL AVERY, CHEMICAL SALESMAN

Nash slides out a driving license then a small portrait photograph of Deborah. He unfolds the press cutting and reads the headline:

SALESMAN MISSING

Below this see the opening words of:

JOE AVERY, A CHEMICAL SALESMAN FROM OAKLAND, FAILED TO RETURN TO HIS HOTEL IN - -

Nash pauses to digest all of this. He then stacks the documents and wallet inside the shoebox and exits.

MAIN LIVING AREA OF TRAILER

Nash pauses about to leave, going back to scan the girlie mags.

MINUTES LATER

Nash focuses keenly on a single page, which he tears out and folds away in a pocket. He collects the shoebox and heads for the door.

INT. BEDROOM - DEBORAH LYING UNCONSCIOUS

Hear the approach of FOOTSTEPS, then POLISHED BROGUE SHOES appear.

A yellow kid-gloved hand reaches and turns Deborah's head casually left to right. A bubble forms on her lips. The gloved hand pinches her cheeks sucking the bubble into her mouth.

                    CREIGHTON (O.S.)
          Oh, dear. Too much for the poor
          darling - -

Creighton's gloved hands reach and take hold of her ankles. He then proceeds to drag her to the big bed, her arms stretching, the towelling robe rides up. Creighton lets her ankles drop and for modesty's sake draws the robe in place. He then snatches a white sheet from off the bed.

Hear the sheet TEAR - -

EXT. GRANT'S TRAILER

As Nash exits, Grant's cheery voice calls out from the darkness:

                    GRANT (O.S.)
          Evenin'.

Nash freezes.

                    GRANT (O.S.)
          All done snoopin' around?

Two gunshot reports split the air. Heavy bullets thud shaking the Trailer, powdered splinters spitting. Nash ducks to his knees, reflexively bringing out his handgun. Grant laughs.

                    GRANT (O.S.)
          Not bad. You got that little
          popgun out real quick, sport - -
          what is it, a DAK? Decent enough
          piece within its limitations.
          Can't say it's gonna be a lot
          of benefit. I could have set two
          zeros double top between your eyes
          no trouble had I wanted. You rate
          as a marksman? I'm what you might
          call a natural in that department.
          Course, it's important to choose
          the right piece. Like my Wildey
          automatic here. Top notch tool,
          real powerhouse. Seven shots to
          the clip, that's all. But then
          it's rare to need more than one.
          Yep, one slug from a Wildey'll
          take the top of your head clean
          off, so it's said.

Nash stares wildly into the darkness. HEADLIGHTS FLASH on the highway for a second, a car, then another, humming, fading to nothing. Nash rakes a glance at the Trailer door. Sweat is beading on his face. He calls out:

                    NASH
          Bowman?

No reply comes back and he tries again.

                    NASH
          You still there?

                    GRANT (O.S.)
          No, I've left and gone on vacation.
            (beat)
          Now where do you suppose I am,
          you brainless prick?

Nash gasps, trying to suppress his panting breathing.

                    NASH
          Bowman? Listen - - you listening?

                    GRANT (O.S.)
          Yeah, I'm all ears.

                    NASH
          You're getting in serious trouble
          here.

                    GRANT (O.S)
          You don't tell me?

He fires off another shot, shaking the Trailer. Nash cowers down. Sweat now
runs freely from his temples.

                    GRANT (O.S.)
          Seems to me it's you what's
          got the trouble, sport.

Another shot. Splinters flying.

                    GRANT (O.S.)
          How you liking it down on your
          knees? Hope you're enjoying it
          as much as I am. Don't bother
          counting shots, by the way. I
          got a whole pile of ammo here.

                    NASH
          Listen to me, Bowman. You hear me?

                    GRANT (O.S)
          Yeah, I hear you. This where you
          tell me we can cut a deal?

                    NASH
          Why not? Okay, you've had your
          fun. Put up your gun and we
          write it off as a gag.

                    GRANT (O.S)
          Like pretend it never happened,
          you mean.

                    NASH
          That's right. But you stop now,
          before things get out of hand.
          I got backup, so don't be a fool.
          I'm giving you a way out.

There is no immediate reply. When Grant speaks again his voice seems to
come from another direction.

                    GRANT (O.S.)
          That's right big of you, sport.
          I truly appreciate it. Only this
          time I'm gonna have to say no.
          That's how my old man dealt with   (CONT'D)

                                                                        82

them travlin blokes what come
around sellin' brushes and stuff.
See I reckon the donkey cart's
gone a mite too far down the road
to consider a peaceable powwow.
Besides, from where I'm standing,
it don't strike me you got a whole
lot to barter with.

                    NASH
Bowman, listen to me - -

                    GRANT (O.S.)
You're a real sly one. Those bibs and
bobs you're clutching for grim death.
What you got in mind to hang me with.
Kind of seals it, wouldn't you say?

                    NASH
Bowman - -

                    GRANT (O.S.)
Hope you don't think I left that
shit lying around willy-nilly. You
can't have rated me that stupid. No
I wanted you to have your minute of
glory. I'm like that, always lookin'
out for the other fella. Could be
frustratin', knowing what you know's
gonna die with you. But like my old
man was fond of saying - - you can't
have everythin' in this life.

                    NASH
Listen to me, Bowman - -

                    GRANT (O.S)
And don't you be frettin' on finding
me a loophole. I got a solid way out
figured for both of us. As for the
backup you mentioned. Good try, sport,
but my gut tells me it ain't so. Sure,
sooner or later the Cavalry will turn
up, bugles soundin'. But by then I'll
be long gone - - and sorry to say, so
will you.

Nash twists his head, searching for an escape.

                    GRANT (O.S.)
What you reckon to the little
lady there? She really is a
spangler, ain't she? And I
swear to Jesus, one sweet lay.

Nash's fear turns to anger, and he calls bitterly:

                    NASH
You're a blackmailer and a
murderer, Bowman. A cop, sworn
to uphold and protect.

                              GRANT (O.S)
                    Thanks for the sermon. You got
                    any prayers, now's the time to
                    say 'em.

Grant fires off a shot. Nash goes down flat, hands covering his head.

Nothing happens. Headlights flash, vehicles hum past on the highway. Nash
uncovers his head and cautiously peers out into the blackness. There is no
sound or movement of any kind. He wipes perspiration from his face. He
waits, puzzling.

He then crams the shoebox under one arm. Headlights flash on the highway
and he reacts. Coming swiftly to his feet, he runs for all he is worth away
from the lighted trailer.

No shots sound. He makes it to a grass bank and goes down flat. He raises
his head and seeing nothing, he scrambles up the bank to the rear of his
parked car.

Nash moves crouching along the car, gun at the ready. He opens the door and
swings inside and turns the ignition, the engine springing to life.

A BLURRED FIGURE - A YELLED SHOUT

Next Nash is being dragged from the car. Grant's big hand fastens on Nash's
gun hand and rips the gun free. Nash throws an instinctive punch.
Bellowing at the top of his lungs, Grant crowds in over Nash, lifts him
with brute strength and hurls him away. Nash hits the ground, going "Ooff!"

The car engine continues to purr. Nash rolls sluggishly, completely winded.
Footsteps crunch and Grant looms above, in no hurry.

                              GRANT
                    You see that movie, *Gladiator?*
                    What we got here is kind of like
                    that. Two big jocks but only one
                    set to get the thumbs up. No prize
                    for guessin' who that's gonna be
                    in this ding-dong.

Nash gives his head a terse shake and struggles to get into a kneeling
position, one foot flat to the ground.

                              GRANT
                    That's the ticket, take your time.
                    Thought I'd give you the chance to
                    show what you're made of.

Nash scrawls up dirt and pebbles. Headlights flash and he pushes upright,
tossing the shards at Grant's face. Grant clumps back, groping at his eyes.

                              GRANT
                    Fuck! Fuck!

Nash follows up, hitting out with both fists. Grant staggers, taking the
blows with ox-like stubbornness, but doesn't fall.

Then with a bellowing shout, he charges at Nash, driving him in a football
tackle, crashing him hard into the car.

                                                                          84

Hands fight for windpipes. Nash gouges at Grant's eyes. Grant twists his head and knocks aside the clawing fingers.

Lights flash and Nash jabs stiff fingers into Grant's throat. Grant makes a harsh squawk, and in fury he grabs a hank of Nash's hair and bashes his head to the cold metal. And holding Nash in position, Grant hauls off and socks him hard on the jaw, draws back and socks again, and again.

Nash sags unconscious. Grant lets him roll off the car to the ground. He staggers back, gasping.

>   GRANT
>   Underestimated you, sport.
>   Made my fuckin' nose bleed.
>   (spits)
>   Might even have busted it.
>   (working at his
>   throat)
>   Hurt my Adam's apple too.
>   Gonna be sore a while.

He coughs harshly and spits again.

>   GRANT
>   But I reckon we know who the
>   top dog is. Yup we got that
>   little matter sorted.

Nash returns to a haze of consciousness. From his p.o.v. see Grant wipe blood from his nose. He coughs and spits some more and steps around to Nash's car, reaches and turns off the ignition and brings out the shoebox. This he kisses and sets on the ground. He opens the car door wide and, muttering, he comes around to where Nash is lying.

Anchoring his feet, Grant gets hold under Nash's armpits and hefts him upright, standing him face to face. He then lowers to hoist Nash in a fireman's lift.

Nash snaps up his knew. Grant screams and grabs at his crotch. Nash hits out desperately. Grant keels but doesn't fall. Nash kicks at Grant's groin, Grant twisting, taking the hit on his hip.

>   GRANT
>   Fuck you to all hell!

Grant piles into Nash. Nash tries to fight back but Grant batters him without mercy, holding him with one and pounding his big fist again and again into Nash's unprotected face.

Grant lets him drop then bears down with all his weight pounding sledgehammer blows repeatedly into Nash's unprotected body. He finally plods back, gasping, wiping a hand across his mouth.

>   GRANT
>   Some pricks never learn.

He follows up and kicks Nash viciously in the ribcage, Nash responding with a moaning sigh. Grant gasps and massages a hand at his gullet. He then takes hold of Nash's jacket lapels and tugs him upright and begins to talk to Nash as if he is conscious and can hear him.

                              GRANT
                    Now. Right down there, sport - -
                    over that ridge - - there's a
                    ravine. Down that slope there.
                    You know the way out I promised?
                    Well this is it. You'll like it
                    down there. Nice and restful.

Grant drags Nash to the open door of the car and heaves him inside. He then
arranges him in a sitting position behind the column and steps back.

Left alone, Nash's head tips limply setting the horn blasting. Grant pulls
him back cutting off the noise. Making a better job of it, he folds Nash's
legs to sit him knees forward, head lolling on his chest.

Grant lowers the window and reaches in and begins working the wheel.

MINUTES LATER

Bowman now has the car pointing the way he wants. He sets on the emergency
brake, gives himself a minute to get his breath. Then reaches in and starts
the engine. He releases the emergency brake and swings the door shut, the
door not quite closing. Grant then bulls his shoulder to the window frame
and starts the car forward.

The car is on a downward slope and as it rolls forward Grant trots to the
rear of the vehicle and pushes from behind, needing to turn and lean back
against the trunk as the car slows, heels digging finding purchase.

As the car picks up momentum, Grant turns again and pushes with main
strength to send it running away toward the ravine.

CAR ROLLING AWAY FROM GRANT

As Grant watches, the car hits a mounded incline and stops.

Assuming the backward position, Grant takes hold of the rear bumper and
brings all his power to jolt the car forward, Grant making a pratfall as it
leaves him.

Grant comes swiftly to his feet to see the car tip into the ravine.

INTERIOR OF NASH'S CAR - THROUGH THE WINDSHIELD

See rapid descent of car.

INTERIOR OF CAR

With the bumping and shaking of the moving car, Nash is brought back to a
hazy wakefulness. From his bleary gaze he registers the danger. Jolting
excessively, the car door swings open and Nash is thrown out.

CAR PLUMMETING DOWNWARD

See it crash head-on to a tree.

TOP OF RAVINE

Grant hears the crash and smirks, going to the edge of the ravine to see
Nash's car wedged to the tree. Grant waits. There is a POP, and a moment
later an ORANGE GLOW spreads around the engine.

Grant's smirk widens into a satisfied grin. He then turns and heads at a smart pace back toward the trailer, stopping to collect the shoebox.

EXHAUSTED PANTING BREATHING

Through foliage pushed aside, see Grant entering the trailer.

MINUTES LATER

Through foliage see Grant emerge hurriedly from the trailer, a big overnight bag in one hand, the shoebox tucked under the other arm.

EXT. TRAILER - CONTINUOUS

Grant heads for his car, opens the door and throws the bag and shoebox inside. He turns to ravine to see distant ORGANGE GLOW, pausing, willing the explosion.

                    GRANT
          Come on, you beaut.

When it fails to happen, Grant makes a 'to-hell-with-it' gesture and swings into the car.

INTERIOR OF GRANT'S CAR

He starts up the engine and gets a CD playing at the same time, Elvis Presley and *Heartbreak Hotel,* the volume at blast level.

Grant revs the engine and drives out from the hollow.

Hear PANTING BREATHING, and from distance see Grant's departing car.

INT. GRANT'S MOVING CAR - HIGHWAY STRETCHING AHEAD

Heartbreak Hotel blasts out. Grant beats his hand at the steering wheel in time with Elvis, his route described through the windshield.

APPROCHING WHITE PILLARS OF DOW ESTATE

Light rain falls, the wipers sweep back and forth on the windshield

OPEN IRON GATES/ WINDING DRIVE

Grant drives through the Gates and continues up the Drive to:

HOUSE

Grant draws to a halt alongside Deborah's sportcar. He cuts the engine, cutting off Elvis at the same time, and gets out. He pauses to consider Deborah's car then turns for the House.

INT. VAST MAIN ROOM

Grant comes into the heart of the room, his gaze settling on:

GIANT PAINTING OF ZACHARY DOW

Grant approaches the painting, staring up. He chuckles.

                              GRANT
                    Move aside you ugly old fucker.

He throws a salute at the picture. He then throws back his head and lets
rip with a cowboy howl:

                              GRANT
                         Ee-haa!

He stops and listens mouth agape as the echo bounces back at him off the
walls. Liking it, he calls out again.

                              GRANT
                    G'day to one and all.

Again the echo comes back, and he follows with a prancing ho-down dance,
going around and around until he spins himself plop down on his behind.
Laughing fit to burst, Grant wobbles upright. He looks up and around.

                              GRANT
                    Now I wonder where she is?

Raises his voice.

                              GRANT
                    You in a playful mood? What do
                    I do, count a slow ten with my
                    eyes closed? Okay, but don't
                    forget I ain't got all night.

He makes to laugh, but the laugh dies as his mood sours. He remembers his
sore Adam's apple and massages at his throat.

                              GRANT
                    Bastard Nash and his fuckin'
                    karate tricks.
                         (coughs and spits)
                    Need a smoke, yeah, a little
                    ciggy.

Saying this, Grant pulls out a crumpled package of Marlboros, strikes a
match on his rump, grinning as it ignites, and lights up.

Spying bottles of spirits set out on a polished table, he pours himself a
king-sized brandy and gets comfortably seated in a big armchair, swigging
brandy and trying for smoke rings.

But his irritable mood persists and he gazes around grumpily.

                              GRANT
                    All this money and all this
                    shit.
                         (suddenly)
                    Fuck it, I've had enough.

He jumps himself upright and strides up on the stage to the big picture
window, staring out to see distant lights glinting.

Tiring of that, he goes to the baby grand piano and pounds out a few
meaningless notes. He takes a last drag and grinds out his cigarette on the
polished wood. The framed portraits set atop the piano catch his attention.

                              GRANT
                    Loada shit!

He sweeps the photographs crashing to the floor. He glowers at the mess and
kicks a foot at it then twists his angry gaze around.

                              GRANT
                    Fuck this.

He downs the remains of the brandy and hurls the glass smash to a wall and
strides away, shouting out:

                              GRANT
                    Where the fuck are you! A
                    game's a game, but I'm in
                    a big hurry.

He starts up the staircase, very determined, calling out:.

                              GRANT
                    You there? You'd better be.
                    You'd better have it waitin'
                    - - and I don't mean pussy.

LANDING/CORRIDOR - LEADING TO MASTER BEDROOM

At the far end of the passage a WEDGE OF LIGHT cuts out as the door to the
Master Bedroom opens - -

                                                          DISSOLVE TO:

EXT. HIGHWAY STRETCHING AHEAD, AS SEEN THROUGH CAR WINDSHIELD - NIGHT

A respectable middle-aged couple sit inside the moving car, the MAN
driving. It is raining and he leans forward to see:

STAGGERING DRUNK

Aware of the approaching car, the Drunk turns and waves but keeps moving.

INTERIOR OF CAR

                         RESPECTABLE MAN
                       (head shaking)
                    Drunk - - can you believe it? Out here.

But his wife sees something very different.

                         RESPECTABLE WOMAN
                    Drive on, Andy! Don't stop!

Andy glances at her but does as told, getting his foot down. The car zooms
past the drunk, who we now see to be Nash.

He plods on, wild-eyed, in the car's wake. He is doubled up in pain. As the
car leaves him, he makes a futile attempt to call out, as DISSOLVE BACK TO:

LANDING/CORRIDOR - WEDGE OF LIGHT CUTTING FROM OPEN DOOR

Grant grins and goes forward, coming to a halt at Carmen's door, beneath
which a CRACK OF LIGHT shows.

Grant debates a second, then grins and turns the doorknob.

                    GRANT
          Anybody home?

No answer comes back as he enters the bedroom. He registers the open valise
and goes up and paws things around. Losing patience, he swats a dismissive
hand and returns to the corridor.

                    GRANT
          Her bad luck.

He heads toward the wedge of light. Reaching the door, he pauses hearing
MUFFLED GRUNTS from inside the room. Grant grins and calls whispering
through the gap:

                    GRANT
          Eager for it again? Got some
          fancy notion in mind?

He pushes the door and goes into:

MASTER BEDROOM

Grant halts. The grin on his face drops, eyes popping, as he sees Deborah.

She stares back at him in terror. A towel has been packed and tied between
her teeth and she kneels propped to the bed trust with strips of torn
sheeting.

Recovering, Grant strolls in and leers down at Deborah, who mutely shakes
her head in warning. Grant snickers uneasily.

                    GRANT
          Now how'd you get done like
          that?

Deborah's wide eyes switch frantically. Grant finally gets the message and
makes to turn, as we hear from behind:

                    CREIGHTON (O.S.)
          Hello, beautiful hunk.

                    GRANT
          Sweet Jesus Christ!

He swings around, open-mouthed. Then rears back, raising a hand in terror
as Creighton's stark white face closes - -

EXT. LONG SHOT OF GATES FRONTING DOW ESTATE - NIGHT

Hear panting breath, feet shuffling as Gates near.

Pull back to see Nash, then follow series of SHORT DISSOLVES as we track
his stumbling progress on DRIVE up to DOORS of HOUSE, HALL, to MAIN ROOM.

See as Nash sees Grant marching with determination toward staircase.

Nash watches Grant mount the Stairs. He then follows. Grant disappears from
view. Nash struggles up the Staircase to:

LANDING/CORRIDOR

Nash sees ahead the OPEN BEDROOM DOOR. Hears Grant SHOUT:

                    GRANT (O.S)
          Sweet Jesus Christ!

HEAR SWISH OF AXE.

Grant SCREAMS, and then more sounds follow, sounds of crashing and falling,
followed by silence.

From the Bedroom, a SING-SONG VOICE LAUGHS OUT.

We see then as Nash sees:

ELGONGATED SHADOW STRETCHING INTO CORRIDOR

The laugh comes again, and from the bedroom:

                    CREIGHTON (O.S.)
          Well, sweetie, we all have to go
          sometime. As they say, here today,
          gone tomorrow. But you had a good
          run - -
             (chuckling)
          For my money.

Nash drags to the open door. Then a WOMAN'S VOICE speaks out, this with a
SPANISH ACCENT:

                    SPANISH WOMAN (O.S.)
          The loco one. He is muerto, Senora.

Nash shakes his head as if unable to believe what he is hearing.

                    SPANISH WOMAN (O.S.)
          But this is not to be regretted. He
          was - how you say? He was the big
          piece of sheet. Though we should
          perhaps have charity in our hearts.
          Perhaps even a peeg such as this one
          deserves to have a prayer said over
          him. This is right, I think. The
          little prayer to send him to the
          hot place below.

She laughs and again we see Nash's disbelief.

A sound then comes from the open door, a STRETCHING, CRACKING SOUND.

                    NEW VOICE (O.S.)
          Now you get it?

Nash grinds shut his eyes as the realization hits him. His eyes snap open
and he bends to peer into the room, to see:

A FIGURE IN TUXEDO

On the floor see a RUBBER MASK. Beyond the Figure, a bound Deborah kneels
staring up in paralyzed fear.

The Figure turns to reveal VERONICA.

She struts, hands-in-pockets, and begins to talking to Deborah.

> VERONICA
> Worked pretty good, wouldn't you
> say? The mask is one of a pair
> me and Creighton wore to go as
> each other at a Halloween party.
> Did you like my Carmen turn? Though
> we should use the bitch's chosen
> name - - Chita Velez. Yeah, Chita,
> the self-styled Mexican vamp. All
> lies, of course. Everything about
> Chita was a lie. She was mostly
> Asian but saw a better future in
> her cha-cha-boom act.

Away to the side, Grant's corpse lies heaped to the wall. On the floor near
him there is a BLOODED AXE.

> VERONICA
> The bitch took it into her head
> to shake me down. Jesus, can you
> believe it, a whore like Chita
> setting out to sharp angle me?
> That's what you get for trying
> to help old pals on the slide.
> See, we used to be lovers - -
> don't look so shocked. Happens
> all the time in our world.

She collects and fluffs a pillow, set it in place.

> VERONICA
> I should have seen it coming. At
> one time she filled in as one of
> Creighton's geisha girls - - not
> for pleasures of the flesh. Well,
> you don't need me to tell you that.
> He just liked to keep raunchy types
> like Chita around for window dressing.
> All history now, but bottom line,
> he moved her out to move me in.

Deborah makes a whimpering sound. Veronica gives her a passing glance and
continues to strut around.

> VERONICA
> She even dragged your smooth
> lawyer into it. Remember Sunday,
> at dinner, when he described my
> last movie? Well my last movie
> just so happens to have been
> Chita's last movie, too. I'd
> guess he was one of her client
> benefactors she had the goods
> on. The poor sap. I fooled him.
> I made out I was Chita. By the
> time he realized, it was too late.

Veronica's head makes an upward snap and begins as if speaking to the air.

                    VERONICA
          Why are you laughing!
              (beat)
          I could act! I could!

Her eyes pop and she grasps at her throat, becoming seized in a sudden violent coughing fit.

Nash sees his chance but is too weakened to take it, watching as Veronica blunders into the glass wardrobe. The retching coughs fade and become distraught bleating sobs. She wipes off her eyes and pushes away from the glass panel and walks to stand menacingly over Deborah.
Again she twists her head and addresses the air.

                    VERONICA
          Then you should have remembered!

She then speaks with the mimicry of Creighton's SING-SONG VOICE.

                    VERONICA
              (SING-SONG)
          Get rid of him for me, Verro - -
          Ple-ease. I can't take any more.

                    VERONICA
              (NORMAL VOICE)
          Is it all coming back? How you hid
          under the table while I applied the
          cushion? Then when it was all over,
          how I had to change you because you
          had messed yourself?

Veronica sways as though dazed, hands clamped to her head.

                    VERONICA
          How cruel you were, Creighton - -
          and so blind! Without money - -
          the money I got for you - - you
          would have been nothing - - nothing!

She swings around mad-eyed to Deborah.

                    VERONICA
          And this one! It wasn't you she
          wanted, you fool! *It was your*
          money!

Her mad eyes fix on the Axe. She seizes it and advances on Deborah.

                    VERONICA
          Are you watching, Creighton!
          This is for you!

She raises the Axe. Deborah cowers back.

Nash crowds in. He grabs Veronica's raised arm with his still functioning right hand pulling her back. She wrenches away.

Nash is unable to hold her. She screams and strikes at him.

The blade hits down on his collarbone, snapping it clean. He cries out, jolting to his knees.

Forgetting Nash, Veronica turns again to Deborah.

She raises the Axe.

Nash rakes at the carpet, grinding his eyes in pain. Through his blurred gaze he sees Veronica standing above Deborah. She has the Axe raised, ready to strike, Deborah cowering.

Nash makes a desperate lunge to fall clumsily over Deborah. He twists and stares up at Veronica, who towers above, legs spread, back arched, for maximum leverage. Her eyes are staring mad woman's eyes.

Nash shakes his head at her.

                    NASH
          No, Veronica.

Veronica freezes, and for the first time she becomes aware of Nash. Her lips move, trying to frame words. Her gaze softens and locks with his. The Axe swings down as if all at once it has become too heavy for her.

                    VERONICA
              (backing away)
          Not you - -

Nash sees Veronica's image shimmer and start to break up. He grinds his teeth to prevent himself blacking out.

Veronica continues to back away, and behind her see:

OPEN DOOR/BANNISTER RAIL

The Axe drops, thudding. Veronica's head tips sideway. Her arms drop limp to her side. Her mouth gapes and her eyes stare out in a glazed hyperthyroid stare.

From deep in her throat a chattering noise emerges. Bubbles foam from her lips as though she is in the first stages of a fit. She wobbles to a halt. Her head begins to rotate.

She is now close to the open door, beyond which is the Bannister Rail.

Veronica begins to back again, stopping, staring up as though hearing Creighton's voice. She clamps her hands over her ears.

                    VERONICA
          Stop! I won't listen!

There is a pause. Her hands drop and she stares up defiantly.

                    VERONICA
          Because you are dead! Because I
          killed you! I wouldn't stay where
          you put me. And now I shall have
          to kill you again!

Another pause, as Veronica appears to be listening.

                    VERONICA/CREIGHTON
                    (SING-SONG)
              Oh, no, Verro. You are not going to
              kill me. I am going to kill you.

Veronica makes a despairing cry, and hissing and spitting, she rages in
fury, clawing at the air. She then begins to tussle, as if with an
invisible force.

Grunting, arms thrust stiffly, palms flatted, she is driven slowly back.

As Nash watches, Veronica thrashes, breaking free.. She wheels around and
tears open the flies of her tux.

                    VERONICA
                    (NORMAL VOICE)
              Here! Take it! I don't want
              it anymore!

Her arm goes back and she throws an object across the room. This lands a
foot or so from Nash and we see as he sees:

CREIGHTON DOW'S DECOMPOSING PENIS

Then Veronica is being driven back again. Fighting with desperation, she
gains a temporary advantage over her phantom assailant.

But the force is too strong. It pushes her through the open door and up to
the Bannister Rail.

Nash sees Veronica being bent backward.

Her head dips out of sight, her body stretching backward over the rail. She
is now toeing the floor, trunk forward, her rammed arms pushing
frantically.

                    VERONICA/CREIGHTON
                    (SING-SONG)
              Together in death, Verro.

Her legs lift and for a moment she balances teetering.

Nash watches helpless to prevent what he can see is about to happen.

Then Veronica slides from the Rail. Her body and legs follow. She does not
scream. Hear CRACK as she hits the lower floor.

Nash stares into the powdery blackness beyond the door.

The world from his p.o.v. starts float as if he is underwater.

Deborah makes a faint murmuring sound, and gritting his teeth, Nash fumbles
out a flat jack-knife. He extracts the blade, needing to use his teeth, and
then saws at the strips of sheeting tying Deborah. She unravels herself the
rest of the way and pulls the gag from out of her mouth.

Nash is slumped over her. She holds his head to her breast, as he mumbles
as sleep blanks him.

                              NASH
                    Got it all wrong - -

FADE

                         THE END

(Note: The ending is felt to be correct, but a CODA tying up the loose
pieces and explaining Veronica's mental distortion can be added if thought
too blunt)